Updated

ESTONIA

Tourist Guide 2023

Unveiling Baltic Charms, Digital Wonders and Rich History – Your Ultimate Travel Companion to Explore the Jewel of Northern Europe

Anya Silver

Table of contents

My first visit to Estonia.................................... 6

CHAPTER 1: INTRODUCTION............................. 9

Why Visit Estonia?.................................... 12

Estonia's Fascinating History....................16

Culture and Traditions............................. 19

Geography and Climate............................23

Quick Facts About Estonia....................... 25

CHAPTER 2: PLANNING YOUR ESTONIAN TRIP 28

Visa and Entry Requirements.................. 28

Best Time to Visit.................................... 31

Travel Budget and Currency.................... 34

Language and Communication................. 37

Safety and Security Tips.......................... 38

Travel Insurance...................................... 42

CHAPTER 3: GETTING TO ESTONIA................. 46

By Air: International Airports.................... 46

Land Borders and Entry Points................48

By Sea: Cruising In.................................. 51

Moving Around Estonia............................ 54

CHAPTER 4: WHERE TO STAY........................... 57

Types of Accommodation..........................57

Best Areas to stay.. 60
How to Get cheap accommodation.......................... 62
Recommended Hotels and Resorts......................... 65
Unique Stays... 73

CHAPTER 5: ESTONIA'S REGIONS AND TOP DESTINATIONS.. **78**
Tallinn.. 78
Tartu..**83**
Pärnu... 89
Saaremaa... 96
Lahemaa National Park..102
Hiiumaa Island...105
Viljandi... 108
Rakvere... 112

CHAPTER 6: ESTONIAN CUISINE AND DINING..
116
Traditional Estonian Dishes................................. 116
Popular Restaurants and Cafés............................. 125

CHAPTER 7: FESTIVALS AND EVENTS IN ESTONIA.. **134**
Song and Dance Celebration................................ 134
Midsummer's Eve (Jaaniõhtu)............................... 135
Tallinn Christmas Market...................................... 136

CHAPTER 8: FUN THINGS TO DO......................142

Hiking and Trekking..................................142

Cycling Adventures..................................143

Water Sports..147

Wildlife Watching....................................151

Winter Sports..151

Island Adventures....................................159

CHAPTER 9: CULTURAL EXPERIENCES.........162

Traditional Estonian Saunas...................163

Folk Music and Dance Performances....................164

Visiting Local Craftspeople....................164

CHAPTER 10: SHOPPING IN ESTONIA.............166

Traditional Craft Markets........................167

Fashion Boutiques..................................168

Design and Souvenir Shops....................169

Shopping Malls..169

Best Places to Shop..................................170

CHAPTER 11: LANGUAGE AND PHRASES BOOK..174

Estonian Pronunciation............................174

Mini Estonian Phrasebook........................175

CHAPTER 12: PRACTICAL TIPS FOR VISITING ESTONIA..180

Electrical Outlets and Voltage..................................180

Internet and Wi-Fi Availability.............................181

Public Toilets and Facilities..................................182

Estonian Traditions and Etiquette.........................183

Health and Medical Information...........................186

Sustainable Travel in Estonia............................... 190

Essential Things To Pack......................................193

CHAPTER 13: TRAVELLING WITH CHILDREN IN ESTONIA...199

Family-Friendly Attractions and Activities...........199

Child Care Facilities... 201

CHAPTER 14: ESTONIA'S UNIQUE TRAITS AND QUIRKS...205

Sauna Culture...205

Singing Revolution...207

Virmalised (Northern Lights)...............................208

APPENDIX...210

Multiple Sample Itinerary....................................210

Regional Map of Estonia's Top Destinations.........220

Useful Websites and Resources............................222

Useful (Android/iOS) Apps.................................224

CONCLUSION...227

My first visit to Estonia

I've always been fascinated by the Baltic states, so when I had the opportunity to visit Estonia for the first time, I was eager to go. I had heard great things about the country's natural beauty, its rich history, and its friendly people.

I arrived in Tallinn, the capital of Estonia, on a sunny spring day. The city was bustling with activity, and I was immediately struck by its beauty. The old town is a UNESCO World Heritage Site, and it's full of mediaeval architecture, cobblestone streets, and charming shops.

I stayed in a small guesthouse in the old town, and I quickly fell in love with my surroundings. My host was a kind and welcoming woman, and she helped me to plan my stay.

One of the first things I did was visit the Kadriorg Palace, which was built in the 18th century by Peter the Great. The palace is surrounded by beautiful gardens, and it's a great place to relax and enjoy the outdoors.

I also visited the Tallinn Town Hall, which is one of the oldest town halls in Europe. The town hall is a beautiful example of Gothic architecture, and it's a must-see for any visitor to Tallinn.

I ate some amazing food during my stay in Estonia. One of my favourite dishes was the Estonian version of the potato pancake, called a "kartupitsapirukas. I also had some of the greatest rye bread I've ever had, as well as some amazing smoked salmon."

The climax of my visit to Estonia was a hike in the Haanja National Park. The park is home to some of the most beautiful scenery in Estonia, and I had a wonderful time hiking among the hills and forests.

I had such a great time in Estonia that I decided to create an updated travel guide for those intending to visit. I wanted to share my love of the country with others, and I wanted to help people plan their own perfect trip to Estonia.

If you're thinking about visiting Estonia, I highly recommend it. The country is a hidden gem, and it has something to offer everyone. From its beautiful natural scenery to its rich history and culture, Estonia is a country that you won't soon forget.

Days	Itinerary

CHAPTER 1: INTRODUCTION

Welcome to the enchanting world of Estonia, a Baltic gem waiting to captivate your heart! Whether you're a curious wanderer, an adventure seeker, or simply in search of a soul-refreshing getaway, Estonia has something magical to offer to each and every traveller.

Picture yourself strolling through the cobbled streets of Tallinn's Old Town, surrounded by mediaeval architecture that seems straight out of a storybook. Feel the warmth of the Estonian hospitality as friendly locals greet you with genuine smiles, inviting you to uncover their land's best-kept secrets.

As you venture beyond the charming capital, a breathtaking natural paradise awaits. Discover the untouched beauty of national parks, where pristine forests and winding trails lead to hidden waterfalls and serene lakes. Embrace the calming embrace of nature and let yourself be swept away by its tranquil embrace.

Estonia is more than just a destination; it's an opportunity to forge unforgettable memories. Indulge in traditional flavours, from hearty stews to sweet pastries, and savour the authentic taste of Estonian cuisine. Delight in centuries-old traditions that come alive through vibrant festivals and captivating events, revealing the soul of a nation proud of its heritage.

Are you a thrill-seeker? Estonia has you covered with a host of outdoor adventures - from cycling through picturesque landscapes to kayaking along the coast, every moment promises excitement and wonder.

But it's not just about the grand experiences; it's the little moments that make Estonia special. Watching the sunset over the Baltic Sea, engaging in heartwarming conversations with locals, or simply pausing to take in the subtle beauty of an ancient forest - these are the moments that weave the fabric of your Estonian journey.

We've crafted this travel guide with love and passion, bringing you the very best Estonia has to offer. Join us as we unlock the secrets of this extraordinary land, where history meets modernity, and where every turn leads to a new discovery.

So, pack your bags, leave your worries behind, and let Estonia work its magic on you. This is more than just a guide; it's an invitation to experience a land of wonder and enchantment. Embrace Estonia, and let your journey of a lifetime begin.

Why Visit Estonia?

Imagine a land where timeless tales come to life, where mediaeval charm meets modern elegance, and where unspoiled nature paints a mesmerising canvas. Welcome to Estonia, a captivating Baltic nation that promises to steal your heart and leave you yearning for more.

So, why visit Estonia? Let me paint a picture for you:

1. Unforgettable Culture and Heritage:

Step into Estonia's enchanting past as you wander through cobblestone streets and historic towns. The well-preserved mediaeval architecture of Tallinn's Old Town is like a living fairytale, inviting you to explore its hidden nooks and winding alleys. Immerse yourself in the lively traditions of the Song and Dance Celebration, where Estonians come together to celebrate their rich heritage.

2. Breathtaking Nature at Your Fingertips:

Nature lovers, rejoice! Estonia boasts an abundance of untouched landscapes that will leave you awestruck. Lose yourself in the tranquillity of national parks, where ancient forests, pristine lakes, and captivating wildlife await. From the picturesque Lahemaa National Park to the serene beauty of Saaremaa Island, every corner reveals a new chapter of Estonia's natural wonder.

3. Warmth of Estonian Hospitality:

Estonians are known for their genuine warmth and welcoming nature. Engage in heartfelt conversations with friendly locals, who will eagerly share their love for their homeland. Experience the joy of being embraced by a community that takes pride in sharing its culture and traditions with open arms.

4. Culinary Delights to Savour:

Taste your way through Estonia's culinary treasures, where hearty flavours and innovative dishes will tantalise your taste buds. Indulge in traditional dishes like mulgikapsad and verivorst, or satisfy your sweet tooth with delectable pastries and marzipan delights. Each bite tells a story of Estonian culture and history.

5. Unique Experiences for Every Traveller:

Estonia offers a diverse array of experiences for every kind of adventurer. Cycle through picturesque landscapes, kayak along the picturesque coast, or witness the beauty of the Northern Lights during the winter months. From urban explorers to nature enthusiasts, there's something for everyone in this versatile destination.

6. A Safe and Peaceful Haven:

Estonia's safety and peace make it an ideal destination for travellers seeking a worry-free escape. Embrace the calm and serenity that permeate this Baltic jewel, knowing that you can explore with ease and comfort.

Estonia is more than just a destination; it's an invitation to a world of wonder, where every moment feels like a cherished memory. Whether you're drawn to its captivating history, enchanted by its nature's beauty, or seeking an off-the-beaten-path adventure, Estonia welcomes you with open arms.

So, why visit Estonia? Because it's a place that beckons your soul and promises an experience that will stay with you forever. Embrace the magic of Estonia, and let your heart guide you to this hidden gem waiting to be discovered.

Estonia's Fascinating History

Step back in time and uncover the captivating story of Estonia's rich and storied past. This Baltic nation's history is like a tapestry, woven with threads of courage, resilience, and determination, making it a fascinating journey worth exploring.

Ancient Roots:

Estonia's history dates back thousands of years, with evidence of human settlement found as far back as 9000 BC. Throughout the ages, various tribes and cultures left their mark on this land, creating a unique blend of traditions and influences.

Mediaeval Marvels:

The mediaeval period shaped Estonia's identity, with the establishment of fortified towns and trading centres along the coastline. Tallinn's Old Town, a UNESCO World Heritage site, is a living testament to this era, boasting mediaeval architecture that transports visitors back in time.

The Teutonic Knights:

In the 13th century, Estonia faced the arrival of the Teutonic Knights, a military order from Germany. The ensuing battles and conquests left a lasting impact on the region's political landscape.

Swedish and Russian Influences:

Over the centuries, Estonia experienced shifts in power, with Swedish and Russian rule leaving indelible marks on the culture and governance of the land. Each era added layers to Estonia's rich tapestry of history.

Independence and Identity:

The 20th century brought both triumphs and challenges for Estonia. After gaining independence following World War I, the country thrived as a democratic republic. However, this newfound freedom was short-lived as the shadow of World War II cast its darkness.

Soviet Occupation and the Singing Revolution:
During the Soviet occupation, Estonia endured hardships and repression. But the spirit of its people remained unbroken. The Singing Revolution of the late 1980s brought a peaceful resistance that eventually led to Estonia's restored independence in 1991.

Estonia's Blossoming Future:
In the modern era, Estonia has blossomed into a forward-thinking and innovative nation. Its advancements in technology and commitment to sustainability have earned it the reputation of a digital pioneer and a leader in environmental conservation.

Today, Estonia's fascinating history is evident in its well-preserved heritage sites, the warmth of its traditions, and the resilience of its people. As you explore this enchanting country, you'll be touched by the spirit of a nation that cherishes its past while embracing the possibilities of the future.

Embrace Estonia's captivating history and let it draw you into its story. From mediaeval charm to contemporary vibrancy, each chapter reveals a land that stands tall against the winds of time. This is a history that continues to shape Estonia's identity and invites you to be a part of its ever-evolving narrative.

Culture and Traditions

In the heart of the Baltics lies a land where culture and traditions weave together to create a mesmerising tapestry. Welcome to Estonia, a place where ancient customs harmonise with modern sensibilities, creating a unique and cherished way of life.

1. Song and Dance: The Rhythm of the Nation

Music and dance are the beating heart of Estonian culture. The Song and Dance Celebration, held every five years, is a grand spectacle that unites the nation in harmony. Thousands of voices rise in unison, singing folk songs that echo the stories of the land. Colourful traditional costumes swirl in time with lively dances, painting a vibrant picture of Estonia's soul.

2. Embracing Nature's Rhythms

Estonians share a profound connection with nature, celebrating the changing seasons and their impact on daily life. The summer solstice, known as "Midsummer's Eve" or "Jaanipäev," is a joyous occasion when bonfires are lit, and families gather to celebrate the white nights. Embrace the timeless tradition of picking wildflowers, weaving them into crowns, and dancing around the bonfire until the early hours.

3. Saunas: A Treasured Ritual

Step into an Estonian sauna, and you'll experience more than just a steam bath. Saunas hold deep cultural significance, acting as a place of cleansing, healing, and camaraderie. Locals embrace this cherished tradition, where shared sauna sessions foster a sense of community and friendship. For a truly authentic experience, venture into a smoke sauna, where the crackling fire and aromatic scents heighten the sense of tranquillity.

4. Marzipan: A Sweet Artistry

Estonia is renowned for its marzipan craftsmanship, where almond confectionery becomes a delightful canvas for artistic expression. Dating back centuries, marzipan has been used to create intricate designs, from whimsical animals to ornate flowers. As you stroll through the charming streets of Tallinn, you'll encounter marzipan masterpieces that are not only delectable but also a testament to Estonian creativity.

5. Handicrafts: Preserving Heritage

Estonians take immense pride in preserving their traditional handicrafts, passing down skills and knowledge through generations. Delicate lacework, intricate wood carvings, and vibrant textiles showcase the artistry of this nation. Treat yourself to a handmade souvenir, and you'll carry a piece of Estonia's cultural heritage with you wherever you go.

6. Warmth of Hospitality

Estonians embody the spirit of hospitality, welcoming visitors with genuine kindness and openness. Experience their warm smiles and willingness to share their culture and traditions. Engaging in conversations with locals provides a glimpse into the soul of Estonia, where stories are exchanged with laughter and heartfelt connections.

Embrace the richness of Estonian culture, where time-honoured traditions blend harmoniously with contemporary living. Immerse yourself in the music, dance, and warmth of the people, and you'll discover a world of beauty and wonder that will leave an indelible mark on your heart. Estonia beckons you to be a part of its cultural tapestry - come, join in the celebration of life and tradition.

Geography and Climate

1. Geography: Estonia is a small country located in Northern Europe, on the eastern coast of the Baltic Sea. It is surrounded by Finland to the north, Latvia to the south, and Russia to the east. Estonia has a total area of 45,227 square kilometres, making it the third-largest country in the Baltics.

The landscape of Estonia is mostly flat, with some hills and forests. There are also over 1,500 islands off the coast of Estonia, including the largest island, Saaremaa. The highest point in Estonia is Suur Munamägi, which is 318 metres (1,043 feet) tall.

2. Climate: Estonia has a temperate climate, with four distinct seasons. The summers are warm and sunny, with average temperatures ranging from 16 to 20 degrees Celsius (61 to 68 degrees Fahrenheit). The winters are cold and snowy, with average temperatures ranging from -4 to -8 degrees Celsius (25 to 18 degrees Fahrenheit).

The climate of Estonia is influenced by its location on the Baltic Sea. The sea moderates the climate, making the winters milder and the summers cooler than they would be if Estonia were located further inland.

3. Rainfall: Estonia receives an average of 568 millimetres (22.3 inches) of precipitation per year. The wettest months are July and August, when the average rainfall is 70-80 millimetres (2.8-3.1 inches). The driest months are February and March, when the average rainfall is 30-40 millimetres (1.2-1.6 inches).

Quick Facts About Estonia

- Capital: Tallinn
- Population: 1.3 million
- Language: Estonian
- Currency: Euro (EUR)
- Time zone: UTC+2
- Border countries: Latvia, Russia, Finland
- Land area: 45,227 square kilometres (17,462 square miles)

- Highest point: Suur Munamägi, 318 metres (1,043 feet)
- Estonia is one of the most digitally advanced countries in the world. Over 99% of government services are available online, and Estonia is a leading country in the use of technology for business and government.
- Estonia was the world's first country to allow its residents to vote online.
- Estonia has the highest number of startups per capita in the European Union.
- Estonia has the world's first e-residency programme, which allows people from all over the world to start and run enterprises without having to live there.
- Estonia has the most saunas per capita in the world. There are an estimated 2 million saunas in Estonia, which is one for every two people.
- Estonia is the birthplace of Skype. Skype was founded in Tallinn in 2003, and it has become one of

the most popular video calling and messaging services in the world.

• Estonia is home to the world's first digital forest. The digital forest is a project that uses sensors to track the health of trees in a forest in Estonia. The data from the sensors is used to help scientists understand how climate change is affecting forests.

Days	Itinerary

CHAPTER 2: PLANNING YOUR ESTONIAN TRIP

Planning your trip here is the first step towards creating cherished memories. Fear not, for I got your back! Let's dive into the details to make this experience as smooth as the smoothest Estonian summer breeze.

Visa and Entry Requirements

Citizens of most countries need a visa to enter Estonia. However, citizens of the following countries can enter Estonia without a visa for up to 90 days:

- European Union countries
- EEA countries
- Switzerland
- Norway
- Iceland

- Liechtenstein
- United States
- Canada
- Australia
- New Zealand

Citizens of other countries can check the visa requirements for Estonia on the website of the Estonian Ministry of Foreign Affairs.

For most travellers, Estonia falls under the Schengen Area, allowing visa-free travel within its member countries.

Entry requirements for Estonia;
In addition to a visa, you will also need to meet the following entry requirements for Estonia:

- A valid passport or travel document
- A return ticket

- Proof of accommodation
- Sufficient financial means to support yourself during your stay

Visa application process:

If you need a visa to enter Estonia, you can apply for one at the Estonian embassy or consulate in your home country. The visa application process can take a few weeks, so it is important to apply well in advance of your trip.

Entry formalities:

When you arrive in Estonia, you will need to go through passport control and customs. You will be required to present your passport and visa to the immigration officer. You may also be asked to show your return ticket and proof of accommodation.

Customs regulations:

You can bring in personal belongings duty-free. However, there are some restrictions on the amount of alcohol and tobacco that you can bring into Estonia. You can find more information about customs regulations on the website of the Estonian Customs Service.

Best Time to Visit

Estonia has a temperate climate, with four different seasons. The summers are warm and sunny, with average temperatures ranging from 16 to 20 degrees Celsius (61 to 68 degrees Fahrenheit). The winters are cold and snowy, with average temperatures ranging from -4 to -8 degrees Celsius (25 to 18 degrees Fahrenheit).

1. Spring (April-May):

Spring is a beautiful time to visit Estonia, as the country comes to life after a long winter. The days are growing longer and the weather is pleasant.

There are also many festivals and events held in Estonia during the spring, such as the Tartu Spring Festival and the Mayflower Days.

2. Summer (June-August):

Summer is the most popular time to visit Estonia, as the weather is warm and sunny. This is the time to enjoy the beaches, go hiking in the forests, and visit the many historical and cultural attractions in Estonia.

3. Autumn (September-October):

Autumn is a great time to visit Estonia if you want to avoid the crowds. The leaves are turning colour and the weather is still good. This is also a good time to go mushroom picking and berry picking.

4. Winter (November-March):

Winter is a magical time to visit Estonia, as the country is covered in snow. This is the time to go skiing, snowboarding, and ice skating. There are also many winter festivals held in Estonia, such as the Pärnu Snow Festival and the Estonian Beer Festival.

Overall, the best time to visit Estonia depends on your interests. If you want to enjoy the beaches and warm weather, then summer is the best time to visit. If you want to avoid the crowds and enjoy the changing leaves, then autumn is a good time to visit. And if you want to experience the magic of winter, then winter is the best time to visit.

Here are some additional things to consider when deciding when to visit Estonia:

• **Festivals:** Estonia has many festivals throughout the year, so if you are interested in attending a festival, you will need to plan your trip accordingly.

- **Events:** Estonia also hosts many sporting events and other events throughout the year. If you are interested in attending an event, you will need to plan your trip accordingly.
- **Weather:** The weather in Estonia can vary depending on the season. If you are sensitive to cold weather, then you may want to avoid visiting Estonia during the winter.
- **Travel costs:** The cost of travel to Estonia can vary depending on the time of year. If you are on a budget, then you may want to avoid visiting Estonia during the peak season (summer).

Travel Budget and Currency

The currency of Estonia is the euro (EUR). One euro is divided into 100 cents. You can exchange your currency for euros at most banks and exchange offices in Estonia.

The cost of travel to Estonia depends on your budget and travel style. However, you can generally expect to spend around €50-€100 per day on a budget. This includes accommodation, food, transportation, and activities.

If you are on a tight budget, you can stay in hostels, eat at budget restaurants, and use public transportation. However, if you are willing to spend more, you can stay in hotels, eat at restaurants, and rent a car.

Here is a breakdown of some of the costs you can expect to incur while visiting Estonia:

- Accommodation: Hostels: €10-€20 per night
- Hotels: €50-€100 per night
- Food: Budget restaurants: €10-€15 per meal
- Restaurants: €20-€30 per meal

- Transportation: Public transportation: €2-€5 per ride
- Rental car: €30-€50 per day
- Activities: Museum entry: €5-€10
- Tours: €20-€30 per person

Tips for budgeting:

- **Book your accommodation in advance:** This will help you get the best deals.
- **Eat at budget restaurants:** There are many affordable restaurants in Estonia where you can get a good meal for a reasonable price.
- **Use public transportation:** Public transportation is a great way to get around Estonia and it is very affordable.
- **Rent a car:** If you want to explore the countryside, renting a car is a good option. However, it is more expensive than public transportation.

- **Do your research:** There are many free or low-cost activities in Estonia. Before you go, find out what is available by doing some findings.

Language and Communication

Language: The official language of Estonia is Estonian. Estonian is a Finno-Ugric language, which means it is related to languages spoken in Finland, Hungary, and Russia. Estonian is a relatively difficult language to learn, but many Estonians speak English, so you should be able to get by without knowing any Estonian.

Communication: If you do not speak Estonian, the best way to communicate with Estonians is in English. Most Estonians speak English at a conversational level, and they are usually happy to help you if you need it.

Here are some tips for communicating with Estonians:

• **Be patient:** Estonians may speak slowly or hesitantly if they are not confident in their English. Be patient with them and let them take their time to speak.

• **Use simple language:** Avoid using complex grammar or vocabulary. Stick to simple words and phrases.

• **Be respectful:** Estonians are a proud people, so be respectful of their culture and language.

Safety and Security Tips

Embarking on a journey to Estonia is an exciting adventure filled with exploration and discovery. To ensure a worry-free experience, it's essential to keep safety and security in mind. So, let me equip you with some valuable tips and emergency numbers to ensure your peace of mind throughout your visit.

1. Stay Aware and Alert:

While Estonia is generally a safe country, it's always wise to stay aware of your surroundings, especially in crowded areas or tourist hotspots. Keep an eye on your belongings, and avoid displaying expensive items that may attract unnecessary attention.

2. Respect the Local Laws and Customs:

Familiarise yourself with the local laws and customs to avoid any unintentional mishaps. Estonia is a country with deep-rooted traditions, and showing respect towards them is appreciated.

3. Use Reliable Transportation:

When travelling within Estonia, opt for licensed and reputable transportation services. Whether it's taxis, public transport, or rental cars, prioritise safety and reliability.

4. Emergency Numbers:

In case of any emergency, keep these essential numbers at hand:

- Police: 112

- Ambulance and Medical Emergencies: 112

- Fire Department: 112

5. Choose Well-Lit and Safe Accommodations:

Select accommodations that prioritise safety and security. Well-lit areas and secure locks add an extra layer of comfort during your stay.

6. Beware of Scams and Petty Crimes:

Be cautious of scams, pickpocketing, and petty crimes, especially in tourist areas. Avoid giving out personal information to strangers or engaging in suspicious activities.

7. Keep Important Documents Secure:

Keep your passport, travel insurance, and other important documents in a secure place, such as a hotel safe or a hidden pouch under your clothes.

8. Drink Responsibly:

If you choose to indulge in Estonia's vibrant nightlife and delicious beverages, do so responsibly. Keep an eye on your drinks and avoid excessive alcohol consumption.

9. Travel Insurance - A Must-Have:

Before travelling to Estonia, ensure you have comprehensive travel insurance that covers medical emergencies, trip cancellations, and other unforeseen situations.

10. Register with Your Embassy:

If you are a foreign traveller, consider registering with your embassy or consulate upon arrival. This helps them assist you in case of any emergencies or critical situations.

11. Weather Precautions:

Estonia experiences varying weather conditions throughout the year. In extreme weather, such as heavy snow or storms, stay updated with weather forecasts and plan accordingly.

12. Trust Your Instincts:

Finally, always make sure to trust your instincts. If you notice unusual and suspicious activities around you, move away from that position or location and seek help if necessary.

Travel Insurance

Travel insurance is not mandatory for visiting Estonia, but it is highly recommended. The cost of travel insurance varies depending on the policy and the length of your trip. However, it is usually a relatively small price to pay for the peace of mind that it can provide.

Travel insurance is a policy that can help cover your costs in case of unexpected events during your trip, such as:

- **Medical expenses:** If you get sick or injured while you're in Estonia, travel insurance can help cover the cost of your medical care.

- **Trip cancellation or interruption:** If you have to cancel or interrupt your trip due to illness, injury, or other unforeseen circumstances, travel insurance can help reimburse you for your non-refundable expenses.

- **Baggage loss or damage:** If your luggage is lost or damaged while you're travelling, travel insurance can help you replace your belongings.

- **Emergency medical transportation:** If you need to be airlifted to a hospital while you're in

Estonia, travel insurance can help cover the cost of the transportation.

When choosing a travel insurance policy, it is important to read the fine print carefully and make sure that the policy covers all of the risks that you are concerned about. You should also make sure that the policy has a high enough limit to cover your potential losses.

Here are some tips for choosing a travel insurance policy:

• **Compare policies from different insurers:** This will help you find the best policy for your needs and budget.

• **Read the fine print:** Make sure that you understand all of the terms and conditions of the policy before you buy it.

- **Ask about exclusions:** Some policies have exclusions for certain risks, such as pre-existing conditions. Make sure that you know what is excluded before you buy a policy.

- **Consider the level of coverage:** The level of coverage that you need will depend on your individual circumstances. If you are travelling to a remote area or participating in risky activities, you may need a higher level of coverage.

- **Get quotes from multiple insurers:** This will help you find the best deal on a policy.

CHAPTER 3: GETTING TO ESTONIA

If Estonia has captured your wanderlust, you're in for a treat! Nestled in the Baltic region, this enchanting country welcomes travellers with open arms. But how do you get there? Well worry not, as we embark on a journey to uncover the various paths that lead to the captivating land of Estonia.

By Air: International Airports

- **Lennart Meri Tallinn Airport:** This is the largest airport in Estonia and is located in the capital city of Tallinn. It is served by a number of airlines, including Air Baltic, Finnair, and SAS.

- **Tartu Airport:** This airport is located in the second largest city of Estonia, Tartu. It is served by a smaller number of airlines, but it is a popular destination for budget airlines.

• **Pärnu Airport:** This airport is located in the third largest city of Estonia, Pärnu. It is a small airport that is only served by a few airlines.

Also remember that, you will need to show your passport and visa when you arrive in Estonia and there are a number of ways to get from the airport to the city centre. You can take a taxi, bus, or train.

There are a number of ways to get cheap flight tickets to Estonia. Here are a few tips:

• **Book your tickets in advance:** This is especially important if you are travelling during the peak season.
• **Be flexible with your travel dates:** If you are flexible with your travel dates, you are more likely to find cheaper tickets.

- **Consider flying into a smaller airport:** If you are willing to fly into a smaller airport, you may be able to find cheaper tickets.
- **Search for deals:** There are a number of websites that offer deals on flights to Estonia.
-

Land Borders and Entry Points

Estonia shares land borders with two countries: Latvia and Russia. There are a number of border crossings between Estonia and these countries, and most of them are open 24 hours a day. However, it is a good idea to check the border crossing hours before you travel, as they may change depending on the time of year.

The main border crossing between Estonia and Latvia is located at Luhamaa. This crossing is on the main highway between Tallinn and Riga. The main border crossing between Estonia and Russia is located at Narva. This crossing is on the main highway between Tallinn and Saint Petersburg.

If you're travelling from neighbouring countries, buses and trains offer convenient and affordable options. The roads are well-maintained, making a road trip an exciting possibility for those seeking the freedom to explore at their own pace.

There are a number of companies that offer bus services to Estonia, including:

• **Lux Express:** Lux Express is the largest bus company in Estonia and offers regular bus services to Estonia from Finland, Latvia, and Russia.

• **Ecolines:** Ecolines is another popular bus company that offers regular bus services to Estonia from Finland, Latvia, and Russia.

- **Nordic Busline:** Nordic Busline is a smaller bus company that offers regular bus services to Estonia from Finland.

The price of a bus ticket to Estonia depends on the company you choose, the time of year you travel, and the type of seat you book. However, you can expect to pay between €20 and €50 for a one-way ticket. You can buy bus tickets to Estonia online, at the bus station, or through a travel agent.

The bus stations in Estonia are open 24 hours a day, 7 days a week. However, the check-in time for buses varies depending on the company you choose.

Here are some tips for getting to Estonia by land:
- **Book your tickets in advance:** This is especially important if you are travelling during the peak season.

- **Check the bus timetable:** Make sure you know the departure and arrival times of your bus.

- **Arrive at the bus station early:** This will give you plenty of time to check in and find your seat.

- **Bring your passport:** You will need your passport to board the bus.

By Sea: Cruising In

For a unique experience, consider arriving by sea. Tallinn's Old Town is a popular destination for cruise ships, offering passengers a breathtaking view of mediaeval spires as they dock. Ferry services from Helsinki, Stockholm, and other neighbouring countries also provide a scenic journey to Estonia's shores.

There are a number of companies that offer ferry services to Estonia, including:

- **Tallink:** Tallink is the largest ferry company in Estonia and offers regular ferry services to Estonia from Finland, Sweden, and Germany.

- **Viking Line:** Viking Line is another popular ferry company that offers regular ferry services to Estonia from Finland and Sweden.

- **DFDS:** DFDS is a Danish ferry company that offers regular ferry services to Estonia from Finland and Sweden.

- **Nordic Jet Line:** Nordic Jet Line is a smaller ferry company that offers regular ferry services to Estonia from Finland.

The price of a ferry ticket to Estonia depends on the company you choose, the time of year you travel, and the type of cabin you book. However, you can expect to pay between €50 and €200 for a one-way ticket.

You can buy ferry tickets to Estonia online, at the ferry terminal, or through a travel agent.
The ferry terminals in Estonia are open 24 hours a day, 7 days a week. However, the check-in time for ferries varies depending on the company you choose.

Here are some tips for getting to Estonia by sea:
• **Book your tickets in advance:** This is especially important if you are travelling during the peak season.

• **Check the ferry timetable:** Make sure you know the departure and arrival times of your ferry.

• **Arrive at the ferry terminal early:** This will give you plenty of time to check in and find your way to your cabin.

- **Bring your passport:** You will need your passport to board the ferry.

Moving Around Estonia

Estonia has a well-developed public transportation system, making it easy to get around the country without a car. The most popular way to get around Estonia is by bus. There is a comprehensive bus network that covers the entire country. Buses are relatively inexpensive and they are a good way to see the countryside.

Another popular way to get around Estonia is by train. There is a less comprehensive train network than buses, but it does cover the major cities and towns. Trains are a bit more expensive than buses, but they are a more comfortable way to travel.

You can as well rent a car in Estonia if you have the budget. This is a good option if you want to explore the countryside at your own pace. However, it is important to note that the roads in Estonia can be narrow and winding, so you should be a confident driver if you choose to rent a car.

There are a number of cheap ways to move around Estonia. Here are a few tips:

• **Use public transportation:** Buses and trains are the cheapest way to get around Estonia.

• **Buy a day pass:** If you are planning on using public transportation a lot in one day, you can buy a day pass. This will save you from spending too much on individual fares.

• **Walk or bike:** If you are staying in a city, you can easily get around by walking or biking. As the doctors will always advise to always go for a walk as a form of exercise, this is also a recommended way to see the city and get some exercise.

• **Share a ride:** There are a number of ride-sharing apps available in Estonia. This is a great way to save money on transportation, especially if you are travelling with a group.

CHAPTER 4: WHERE TO STAY

Wherever you decide to stay in Estonia, you'll find warm hospitality, rich history, and picturesque surroundings to make your visit truly special. Whether it's a boutique hotel in Tallinn's old town, a guesthouse on Saaremaa Island, or a countryside retreat in Lahemaa National Park, Estonia's accommodations promise a comfortable and immersive experience. So, choose your perfect home away from home, and let Estonia's magic weave its enchanting spell around you!

Types of Accommodation

There are a number of different types of accommodation available in Estonia, to suit all budgets and preferences. Here are a few of the most go to options available:

1. Hotels: Hotels are the most common type of accommodation in Estonia. They offer a variety of amenities, including room service, laundry service, and Wi-Fi.

2. Hostels: Hostels are a preferred choice for budget travellers and backpackers. They offer shared rooms and bathrooms, and they are often located in central locations.

3. Apartments: Apartments are a good option for travellers who want more privacy and space. They can be rented by the week or the month, and they often come with kitchenettes.

4. Campgrounds: Camping is a great option for travellers who want to experience the outdoors. There are a number of campgrounds located throughout Estonia, and they offer a variety of amenities, including showers, laundry facilities, and Wi-Fi.

5. Bed and breakfasts: Bed and breakfasts are a great option for travellers who want a homestay experience. They offer private rooms and breakfast, and they are often located in charming villages.

Here are some tips for choosing accommodation in Estonia:

• **Consider your budget:** Accommodation prices in Estonia vary depending on the type of accommodation you choose and the time of year you travel.

• **Think about your location:** If you want to be close to the city centre, you will need to pay more for accommodation. If you are happy to stay in a more rural location, you can find cheaper accommodation.

• **Book in advance:** If you are travelling during peak season, it is a good idea to book your accommodation in advance. This will enable you get the best possible deal before your trip.

Best Areas to stay

Estonia is a small country with a lot to offer visitors. There are a number of great places to stay, depending on your interests and budget. Here are a few of the best areas to stay in Estonia:

1. Tallinn: The capital of Estonia, Tallinn is a charming city with a rich history. It is home to many historical landmarks, including the Old Town, which is a UNESCO World Heritage Site. There are also a number of museums, art galleries, and restaurants in Tallinn.

2. Tartu: The second largest city in Estonia, Tartu is a university town with a lively atmosphere. It is home to a number of museums, theatres, and concert halls. There are also a number of parks and green spaces in Tartu.

3. Pärnu: A popular seaside resort town, Pärnu is known for its beaches, spas, and nightlife. It is also home to a number of historical landmarks, including the Pärnu Town Hall and the Pärnu Cathedral.

4. Haapsalu: A beautiful town located on the coast of the Gulf of Finland, Haapsalu is known for its mediaeval castle and its thermal springs. It is also a popular destination for hiking, biking, and sailing.

5. Kuressaare: The capital of Saaremaa, the largest island in Estonia, Kuressaare is a charming town with a well-preserved Old Town. It is home to a number of museums, art galleries, and restaurants. There are also a number of beaches and nature reserves in the area.

Here are some factors to consider when choosing an area to stay in Estonia:

- **Your interests:** If you are interested in history, you might want to stay in Tallinn or Tartu. If you are interested in nature, you might want to stay in Pärnu or Haapsalu.
- **Your budget:** Accommodation prices in Estonia vary depending on the area. If you are on a budget, you might want to stay in a hostel or a bed and breakfast.
- **The time of year:** If you are travelling during peak season, it is a good idea to book your accommodation in advance. Doing this will make sure you get the best deal possible.

How to Get cheap accommodation

1. Stay in a hostel: Hostels are a great option for budget travellers. They offer shared rooms and bathrooms, and they are often located in central locations.

2. Stay in a bed and breakfast: Bed and breakfasts are a great option for travellers who want a homestay experience. They offer private rooms and breakfast, and they are often located in charming villages.

3. Camp in a campground: Camping is a great option for travellers who want to experience the outdoors. There are a number of campgrounds located throughout Estonia, and they offer a variety of amenities, including showers, laundry facilities, and Wi-Fi.

4. Rent an apartment: Apartments are a good option for travellers who want more privacy and space. They can be rented by the week or the month, and they often come with kitchenettes.

5. Stay in a rural area: Accommodation prices are generally lower in rural areas than in urban areas. If you are willing to stay outside of the city centre, you can find some great deals.

6. Book your accommodation in advance: If you are travelling during peak season, it is a good idea to book your accommodation in advance. Doing this will make sure you get the best deal possible.

7. Look for deals and discounts: There are a number of websites and apps that offer deals and discounts on accommodation in Estonia. Do some research before you book to see if you can find a good deal.

Here are some additional tips for getting cheap accommodations in Estonia:

- **Be flexible with your dates:** If you are flexible with your travel dates, you are more likely to find cheaper accommodation.

- **Consider staying in a shared room:** If you are on a tight budget, you can save money by staying in a shared room.

- **Look for hostels that offer free breakfast:** Some hostels offer free breakfast, which can save you money on food costs.

- **Cook your own meals:** If you are on a tight budget, you can save money by cooking your own meals.

- **Take advantage of free activities:** There are a number of free activities available in Estonia, such as hiking, biking, and swimming.

Recommended Hotels and Resorts

Estonia offers a wide range of accommodations that cater to every traveller's preferences. Whether you seek luxurious hotels, cozy hostels, or serene resorts, Estonia has something special in store for you. Let's explore some of the recommended places to stay, their unique features, approximate prices, and stunning locations.

1. Tallinn - The Medieval Marvel

• Hotel Telegraaf (Location: Vene 9, Tallinn Old Town)

- A 5-star luxury hotel in the heart of Tallinn's Old Town.

- Features elegantly designed rooms, spa facilities, and a rooftop terrace.

- Approximate Price Range: €140 - €300 per night.

• Euphoria Hotel (Location: Nunne 4, Tallinn Old Town)

- A boutique hotel with a blend of modern design and historic charm.

- Offers spacious rooms, a stylish bar, and a central location.
- Approximate Price Range: €100 - €200 per night.

- Red Emperor Hostel (Location: Kuninga 1, Tallinn Old Town)
- A budget-friendly hostel with a lively atmosphere.
- Provides shared and private rooms, a communal kitchen, and a social lounge.
- Approximate Price Range: €15 - €50 per night.

- Radisson Blu Hotel Olümpia is a 4-star hotel also located in Tallinn, and it is just a short walk from the Viru Gate, one of the most famous landmarks in the city. Prices start at €150 per night.

- The Guild is a 5-star hotel located in the heart of Tallinn, just steps from the Old Town. It has a rooftop bar where you can enjoy stunning views of the city while you sip some drinks. Prices start at €300 per night.

• Tallink Hotel Viimsi Spa is a 4-star hotel located in Viimsi, just outside of Tallinn. It has a spa with a variety of treatments and a private beach. Prices start at €140 per night.

• Meriton Old Town Hotel is a 4-star hotel located in the heart of Tallinn's Old Town, and it is just a short walk from many of the city's top attractions. Prices start at €100 per night.

• Tallinn Backpackers is also located in Tallinn, and it is just a short walk from the Viru Gate. Prices start at €30 per night for a dorm bed.

• Red Emperor Hostel is a hostel located in the heart of Tallinn, and it is just a short walk from the

Old Town. Prices start at €25 per night for a dorm bed.

• Hostel Old Town is located in the heart of Tallinn's Old Town, and it is just a short walk from many of the city's top attractions. Prices start at €20 per night for a dorm bed.

2. Tartu - The Student City

• Dorpat Hotel & Convention Centre (Location: Soola 6, Tartu)

- A well-established hotel with comfortable rooms and conference facilities.

- Boasts a riverside location and proximity to the city's main attractions.

- Approximate Price Range: €80 - €150 per night.

• Hektor Container Hotel (Location: Riia 26, Tartu)

- A unique and eco-friendly hotel made from repurposed shipping containers.

- Offers compact yet stylish rooms and a trendy café.
- Approximate Price Range: €50 - €100 per night.

• Academus Hostel (Location: Yeturu 5, Tartu)
- A cozy and friendly hostel in the heart of Tartu.
- Provides dormitory-style rooms and a communal kitchen.
- Approximate Price Range: €15 - €40 per night.

• Hestia Hotel Ilmarine is a 4-star hotel located in Tartu, and it is just a short walk from the University of Tartu. Prices start at €100 per night.

• Alexander Hotel is a 4-star hotel located in Tartu, and it is just a short walk from the University of Tartu. Prices start at €100 per night.

• Kristine's Guesthouse is located in Tartu, and it is just a short walk from the University of Tartu. Prices start at €25 per night for a private room.

3. Pärnu - The Beachside Haven

- Strand Spa & Conference Hotel (Location: A.H. Tammsaare pst 35, Pärnu)

- A beachfront hotel with modern amenities and spa facilities.

- Offers comfortable rooms, a pool, and it has direct access to the beach.

- Approximate Price Range: €80 - €180 per night.

- Villa Ammende (Location: Mere puiestee 7, Pärnu)

- A historic villa turned boutique hotel with a touch of elegance.

- Features beautifully decorated rooms, a gourmet restaurant, and a lush garden.

- Approximate Price Range: €150 - €300 per night.

- Seedri Apartments (Location: Seedri 6, Pärnu)

- Self-catering apartments perfect for families or groups.

- Provides spacious and well-equipped units with a home-away-from-home feel.

- Approximate Price Range: €70 - €150 per night.

• Noorus Spa Hotel & Conference Centre is a 4-star hotel located in Pärnu, and it has a spa with a variety of treatments. Prices start at €150 per night.

• Sleep Well Hostel is a hostel located in Pärnu, and it is just a short walk from the beach. Prices start at €20 per night for a dorm bed.

4. Saaremaa - The Island Oasis

• Georg Ots Spa Hotel (Location: Kuressaare, Saaremaa)

- A relaxing spa hotel with a scenic coastal setting.

- Offers comfortable rooms, spa treatments, and an indoor pool.

- Approximate Price Range: €80 - €150 per night.

• Padaste Manor (Location: Muhu Island, Saaremaa)

- A luxurious manor hotel surrounded by nature.

- Provides elegant rooms, gourmet dining, and a tranquil atmosphere.

- Approximate Price Range: €200 - €500 per night.

• Kuressaare Linnahotell (Location: Tallinna 15, Kuressaare)

- A charming hotel in the heart of Kuressaare, Saaremaa's capital.

- Features cozy rooms and a restaurant with local specialties.

- Approximate Price Range: €60 - €120 per night.

• Meri&TerraSpa Hotel is a 4-star hotel located in Kuressaare, and it has a spa with a variety of treatments. Prices start at €120 per night.

Unique Stays

1. Farmstay: Estonia is a great place to experience farm life, and there are a number of farmstays located throughout the country. These stays offer guests the opportunity to learn about traditional Estonian farming practices, as well as to enjoy fresh, local food.

Some of the most popular farmstays in Estonia include:

• Koidula Talu is a working farm located in the Võru County. Guests can help out with the farm chores, such as feeding the animals and collecting eggs. They can also enjoy traditional Estonian food, such as black bread and kohuke (curd cheese).

• Lahemaa Farm is a family-run farm located in the Lahemaa National Park. Guests can enjoy hiking, biking, and fishing on the farm's grounds. They can also learn about traditional Estonian handicrafts, such as weaving and pottery.

- Ranna Rantšo is a working farm located in the Pärnu County. Guests can enjoy horseback riding, swimming, and fishing on the farm's grounds. They can also learn about traditional Estonian animal husbandry.

2. Guesthouses: Estonia also has a number of charming guest houses located in rural areas. These guesthouses offer guests a more intimate and personal experience than hotels. They often have a homey atmosphere, and they are often located in beautiful settings.

Some of the most popular guesthouses in Estonia include:

- Mäetaguse Manor is a 19th-century manor house located in the Ida-Viru County. The manor house has been converted into a guesthouse, and it offers guests elegant rooms, as well as access to the manor's gardens and forests.

- Kärdla Guesthouse is a family-run guesthouse located on Hiiumaa Island. The guesthouse is located in a traditional Estonian farmhouse, and it offers guests simple but comfortable rooms. Guests can also enjoy hiking, biking, and fishing on the island.

- Rannarahva Villa is a guesthouse located in the Pärnu County. The guesthouse is located on the coast, and it offers guests stunning views of the Baltic Sea. Guests can also enjoy swimming, sunbathing, and hiking on the beach.

3. Camping: Estonia is also a great place to go camping, and there are a number of campsites located throughout the country. These campsites offer guests a variety of facilities, such as showers, toilets, and laundry facilities. They also often have a playground, a swimming pool, and a sauna.

Some of the most popular campsites in Estonia include:

• Lahemaa National Park is a national park located in the north-west of Estonia. The park has a number of campsites, including a campsite located on the coast.

• Pärnu Bay is a bay located in the south-west of Estonia. The bay has a number of campsites, including a campsite located on the beach.

- Saaremaa is an island located in the west of Estonia. The island has a number of campsites, including a campsite located in the island's national park.

CHAPTER 5: REGIONS AND TOP DESTINATIONS

Estonia, a captivating country nestled in the Baltic region, offers a treasure trove of diverse landscapes and cultural wonders. Each region boasts its own unique charm and top destinations that are waiting to be explored. Let's embark on a journey through Estonia's regions and discover its top destinations that will leave you enchanted.

Tallinn

Welcome to Tallinn, the captivating capital of Estonia, where ancient history meets modern creativity. This charming city offers a wealth of experiences that will leave you enchanted and inspired. Let's delve into the top attractions that make Tallinn a must-visit destination.

Tallinn's Old Town - A Medieval Marvel

Step back in time as you explore Tallinn's Old Town, a UNESCO World Heritage Site that takes you on a journey through centuries of history. Wander through cobbled streets lined with picturesque merchant houses and mediaeval towers. Town Hall Square stands at the heart of this enchanting district, where you'll find historic buildings adorned with ornate facades. Immerse yourself in the lively atmosphere, as the square comes alive with cafes, restaurants, and local markets.

Toompea Hill - Panoramic Views and Ancient Legends

Climb Toompea Hill to reach the upper town, where panoramic views of Tallinn and the Baltic Sea await. This historic area is home to the Estonian Parliament and the stately Alexander Nevsky Cathedral, an architectural marvel adorned with intricate onion domes. Legend has it that Toompea Hill was created by the ancient hero Kalev, who is said to have been buried here. Explore the mysterious tunnels beneath the hill, known as the Kiek in de Kök, to unravel more of Tallinn's intriguing history.

Kadriorg Park and Palace - Nature's Oasis of Elegance

Find solace in the beauty of Kadriorg Park and Palace, a serene oasis nestled amidst the city's hustle and bustle. This splendid Baroque palace, built by Peter the Great for his empress Catherine I, exudes elegance and grandeur. Stroll through the meticulously landscaped gardens adorned with fountains and sculptures, offering a tranquil escape from urban life. The park is also home to the Kadriorg Art Museum, housing an impressive collection of foreign art from the 16th to 20th centuries and the Kumu Art Museum.

Telliskivi Creative City - Where Art and Innovation Converge

For a taste of Tallinn's contemporary creativity, head to Telliskivi Creative City, a vibrant hub for artists, designers, and entrepreneurs. Formerly an industrial complex, this area has been transformed into a lively cultural hotspot. Explore the numerous art studios, galleries, and trendy shops showcasing local talent. The creative atmosphere is infectious, and you'll find yourself drawn to the unique blend of art, food, and design that fills the air.

Other must-visit destinations in Tallinn that will intrigue and wow visitors include:

- **Toompea Castle:** Toompea Castle is a mediaeval castle located on Toompea Hill, the highest point in Tallinn. The castle has been the seat of the Estonian Parliament since 1919 and is a popular tourist destination.

- **Lennusadam Seaplane Harbour:** Lennusadam Seaplane Harbour is a former seaplane harbour that is now a museum. The museum is home to a number of exhibits on the history of seaplanes and Estonian maritime history.

- **St. Olav's Church:** St. Olav's Church is a 13th-century church located in the Old Town. The church is the tallest building in Tallinn and offers stunning views of the city.

- **Kiek in de Kök:** Kiek in de Kök is a 15th-century tower that was part of the city's fortifications. The tower is now a museum and offers panoramic views of the city.

- **Pirita Beach:** Pirita Beach is a popular beach located in the north of Tallinn. The beach is a great place to relax, swim, or sunbathe.

Tallinn is a city of contrasts, where mediaeval charm intertwines with modern innovation. From the timelessness of the Old Town to the creativity of Telliskivi Creative City, each corner of Tallinn offers a unique experience waiting to be discovered. Whether you immerse yourself in the rich history of Toompea Hill or find serenity in the elegance of Kadriorg Park, Tallinn promises to leave you with cherished memories and a deeper appreciation for Estonia's cultural heritage. Embrace the magic of Tallinn and let this captivating city weave its enchanting spell around you.

Tartu

I call Tartu, the intellectual soul of Estonia, where history, nature, and creativity converge to create a captivating experience. There are many different top destinations in Tartu that are worth visiting, including:

University of Tartu - Nurturing Knowledge and Tradition

Immerse yourself in the rich academic heritage of Tartu by visiting the esteemed University of Tartu. Founded in 1632, it is one of the oldest and most prestigious universities in Northern Europe. The university's main building, adorned with neoclassical architecture, stands tall as a symbol of knowledge and enlightenment. Take a stroll through its historic halls and picturesque courtyards, where generations of scholars have sought wisdom and inspiration.

Tartu Old Town - A Timeless Tapestry of History

Step into the past as you explore Tartu's Old Town, a captivating district steeped in history and charm. Stroll along narrow cobblestone streets adorned with colourful merchant houses and mediaeval architecture. Raekoja plats, the central square, is the heart of the Old Town, surrounded by historical landmarks, cafes, and boutiques. Visit the iconic Tartu Town Hall, a striking blend of Gothic and Baroque styles, and the historical St. John's Church, which has watched over the town since the 14th century. Discover the storytelling statues that bring legends and myths to life, adding a touch of whimsy to this time-honoured tapestry.

Emajõgi Riverfront - A Riverside Haven

The tranquil Emajõgi Riverfront offers a serene escape from the city's hustle and bustle. Stroll along the scenic riverbanks, where nature's beauty harmonises with urban life. The riverfront is a beloved gathering place for locals and visitors alike, with parks, promenades, and charming cafes lining the water's edge. Rent a bike and explore the river's picturesque pathways or embark on a relaxing boat trip to appreciate Tartu from a different perspective. In summer, the riverfront comes alive with open-air concerts, festivals, and outdoor events, adding to the city's vibrant atmosphere.

Other top destinations in Tartu that you will really find fun and interesting include:

• **Science Centre AHHAA:** The Science Centre AHHAA is a popular tourist destination for families with children. It has over 250 interactive exhibits that explore science and technology in a fun and engaging way.

• **Tartu University Botanical Garden:** The Tartu University Botanical Garden is one of the oldest botanical gardens in Europe. It is home to over 10,000 plant species, and it is a popular spot for hiking, biking, and picnicking.

• **Tartu Toy Museum:** The Tartu Toy Museum is a great place to learn about the history of toys. It has a collection of over 12,000 toys from around the world, and it offers a variety of educational activities for children.

- **St. John's Church:** St. John's Church is a Lutheran church that was built in the 14th century. It is one of the most important historical buildings in Tartu, and it offers stunning views of the city from its bell tower.

- **Toomemägi Park:** Toomemägi Park is a hilltop park that offers stunning views of Tartu. It is home to the ruins of Tartu Cathedral, as well as the University of Tartu's main building.

- **Emajõgi River:** The Emajõgi River is a major river that flows through Tartu. It is a well known location for swimming, boating and fishing.

In addition to these popular tourist destinations, there are many other great places to visit in Tartu. Here are a few more suggestions:

- **The Estonian National Museum:** The Estonian National Museum is a great place to learn about the history and culture of Estonia. It has a collection of over 800,000 artefacts, and it offers a variety of educational activities for visitors of all ages.

- **The Tartu Art Museum:** The Tartu Art Museum is a great place to see Estonian art from the 18th century to the present day. It has a collection of over 10,000 works of art, including paintings, sculptures, and drawings.

- **The Supilinn District:** The Supilinn District is a charming neighbourhood in Tartu that is known for its wooden houses and its laid-back atmosphere.

It is a great place to wander around and explore the local shops and cafes.

• **The Tartu Market:** The Tartu Market is a great place to buy fresh produce, meats, and cheeses. It is also a great place to sample Estonian food from different regions of the country.

• **The Tartu Christmas Market:** The Tartu Christmas Market is a popular tourist destination during the holiday season. It is a great place to buy Christmas ornaments, gifts, and food.

Pärnu

I call Pärnu, the summer capital of Estonia, where sun-kissed beaches, rich history, and vibrant culture come together to create an unforgettable experience. Pärnu is a city in southwestern Estonia that overlooks Pärnu Bay. It is well-known for its long sandy beach, various restaurants, cocktail bars, spas, and laid-back atmosphere. Pärnu is Estonia's largest municipality, with an area of 858 km2, almost as large as Berlin (892 km2). Let's explore the top attractions that make Pärnu a beloved destination for travellers from near and far.

Pärnu Beach - The Seaside Paradise

Pärnu's pristine sandy beach is a true oasis for beach lovers and water enthusiasts alike. Stretching along the Gulf of Riga, the beach beckons with its gentle waves and soft golden sands. Bask in the sun's warm embrace, take refreshing dips in the sea, or build sandcastles with loved ones. The beachfront promenade invites leisurely strolls and is dotted with cafes, ice cream stands, and charming boutiques. In the summer, the beach becomes a hub of activity, with beach volleyball tournaments, water sports, and live music events adding to the festive atmosphere. Pärnu Beach is the perfect place to unwind, recharge, and embrace the carefree spirit of summer.

Pärnu Museum - Unravelling the City's Past

Delve into Pärnu's rich history and cultural heritage at the Pärnu Museum, located in a beautifully restored historic granary. The museum offers a captivating journey through the city's past, showcasing artefacts, photographs, and interactive exhibits that bring history to life. Discover the town's maritime legacy, learn about the region's ancient roots, and explore the impact of various historical periods on Pärnu's development. The museum's comprehensive displays offer insight into the town's evolution from a mediaeval trading hub to a popular resort destination. With its engaging presentations, the Pärnu Museum promises an informative and immersive experience for history enthusiasts and curious travellers alike.

Endla Theatre - Where the Arts Flourish

Embrace the vibrant arts scene of Pärnu at the Endla Theatre, a cultural gem that delights audiences with a diverse repertoire of performances. Established in 1906, the theatre has a storied history and a strong tradition of nurturing local talent. From captivating drama to enthralling musical performances, the Endla Theatre offers a range of shows that cater to various tastes and interests. Join in the applause for acclaimed actors and musicians, and witness the magic of live performances in this cozy and charming venue. The Endla Theatre is not just a cultural institution, but a reflection of the city's creative spirit and a source of inspiration for the community.

Pärnu Old Town - A Timeless Beauty

Step back in time as you wander through the historic Pärnu Old Town, a picturesque district adorned with colourful buildings and charming cobblestone streets. Raekoja plats, the town's central square, is the heart of the Old Town and exudes a lively ambiance with its cafes, restaurants, and local markets. Discover architectural gems like the striking Town Hall and the historic St. Catherine's Church. Admire the town's storytelling statues, which bring legends and folklore to life. The Old Town's quaint shops, galleries, and boutiques offer unique souvenirs and treasures to take home as mementos of your Pärnu experience.

Rannapark - Nature's Tranquil Retreat

For a serene escape amid nature, head to Rannapark, a lush green oasis nestled between Pärnu Beach and the town centre. This peaceful park provides an idyllic setting for a leisurely stroll, a relaxing picnic, or simply unwinding in the embrace of nature. The park's winding pathways, lovely flowerbeds, and tall trees create a tranquil ambiance that invites you to slow down and savour the moment. Take a seat by the ornate fountain or find solace under the shade of a tree, and let the tranquil surroundings rejuvenate your senses.

Pärnu Mud Baths - Health and Wellness

Pärnu is renowned for its therapeutic mud baths, which have been treasured for their healing properties for centuries. Treat yourself to a soothing mud bath experience at one of the town's reputable spas, where you can indulge in a wellness ritual that combines natural mud treatments with relaxing massages. The warm and mineral-rich mud is believed to have various health benefits, promoting relaxation, improved circulation, and the rejuvenation of skin. Embrace the restorative powers of Pärnu's mud baths and emerge feeling revitalised and refreshed.

Pärnu Vallikäär - The Historic City Wall

Explore Pärnu's rich mediaeval heritage by visiting Pärnu Vallikäär, the town's historic city wall. Built in the 17th century, the well-preserved fortifications offer glimpses into the town's defensive past. Take a leisurely walk along the wall's impressive ramparts, which provide a unique vantage point to appreciate the town's layout and surrounding landscapes. The Vallikäär is not just a historical site but also a recreational area, offering pleasant walking and biking paths, as well as green spaces where locals and visitors can enjoy outdoor activities.

Other top destinations in Pärnu worth visiting include;

● **Tervise Paradiis Water Park:** Tervise Paradiis is a large water park with a variety of slides, pools, and saunas. It is a great place to cool off on a hot day or to have some fun with the family.

- **Lottemaa Theme Park:** Lottemaa is a theme park based on the popular Estonian children's book character Lotte. The park has a variety of rides, shows, and attractions, making it a great place for families with children.

Pärnu, the sun-kissed gem of Estonia, offers a blend of sun-soaked beaches, historical intrigue, and artistic delights. Pärnu Beach beckons with its inviting waters and lively ambiance, providing the perfect setting for leisure and relaxation. Whether you seek sun and sea, historical insights, or artistic inspiration, Pärnu promises to leave you with cherished memories and a deeper connection to Estonia's coastal beauty.

Saaremaa

Saaremaa is the largest island in Estonia, and it is known for its beautiful nature, rich history, and charming towns. Saaremaa's top destinations promise a journey of enchantment and discovery. Let's embark on a comprehensive exploration of the island's captivating treasures.

Kuressaare - The Island's Charming Capital

Begin your Saaremaa adventure in Kuressaare, the island's capital and a town steeped in history. Kuressaare Castle, dating back to the 14th century, stands as an iconic symbol of the island's past. Wander through its ancient walls and discover the castle's intriguing history in the museum housed within. Stroll along the picturesque streets of Kuressaare, adorned with charming wooden buildings and cozy cafes. The town's peaceful ambiance invites you to unwind and embrace the slower pace of island life.

Kaali Meteorite Crater - A Celestial Wonder

Explore the awe-inspiring Kaali Meteorite Crater, a rare natural wonder created by a meteorite impact thousands of years ago. The main crater, surrounded by smaller ones, offers a glimpse into the island's geological history. The site is steeped in ancient myths and legends, adding to its mysterious allure. Take a walk around the crater and imagine the extraordinary event that shaped the landscape.

Muhu Island - Tranquil Serenity

Connected to Saaremaa by a causeway, Muhu Island invites you to experience a tranquil retreat. Discover the idyllic charm of the island's countryside, dotted with traditional farmhouses and breathtaking coastal views. Visit the Muhu Museum to learn about the island's rich cultural heritage and folklore. Explore Koguva Village, a well-preserved fishing village, and immerse yourself in the authenticity of rural island life.

Saaremaa Windmills - Iconic Landmarks

As you journey through Saaremaa's countryside, you'll encounter the iconic windmills that have become symbols of the island's rural charm. These wooden structures, some dating back centuries, showcase the island's historical dependence on wind power. Discover windmills in places like Angla and Triigi, where you can learn about the milling process and admire the traditional architecture.

Panga Cliff - Nature's Majesty

Witness the majestic beauty of Panga Cliff, where the Baltic Sea's waves crash against towering limestone cliffs. The panoramic views from the cliff's edge are awe-inspiring, offering a captivating vantage point to observe the sea's raw power. Panga Cliff is a paradise for nature lovers and photographers, especially during sunset when the sky and sea blend in a stunning display of colours.

Vilsandi National Park - A Nature Lover's Paradise

Step into the unspoiled wilderness of Vilsandi National Park, a protected area of diverse landscapes and abundant wildlife. Explore the park's network of nature trails and bird watching towers, ideal for observing migratory birds and local wildlife. Vilsandi's coastal beauty and serene atmosphere make it a perfect destination for nature enthusiasts and those seeking solitude in nature.

Other top destinations worth visiting in Saaremaa include:

• **Saaremaa Museum:** This museum is located in Kuressaare, and it tells the story of Saaremaa's history and culture. You can see exhibits on the island's prehistoric inhabitants, its mediaeval history, and its role in the Estonian War of Independence.

- **Järve Beach:** This beach is one of the most popular beaches in Saaremaa, and it is known for its white sand and clear waters. You can swim, sunbathe, or go for a walk along the beach.

- **Sõrve Lighthouse:** This lighthouse is located at the southern tip of Saaremaa, and it offers stunning views of the Baltic Sea. You can climb to the top of the lighthouse for panoramic views of the surrounding area.

These are just a few of the many top destinations in Saaremaa. With its beautiful scenery, rich history, and charming towns, Saaremaa is a great place to visit for a relaxing vacation or an exciting adventure.

In addition to these popular destinations, there are many other things to see and do in Saaremaa. You can go hiking or biking in the forests, visit the many farms and manor houses, or take a boat trip to one of the island's many islets. There are also plenty of opportunities to try local food and drink, such as the island's famous smoked fish and beer.

Lahemaa National Park

Lahemaa National Park is the largest national park in Estonia, and it is located in the north of the country. The park covers an area of 747 square kilometres, and it includes a variety of different landscapes, including forests, bogs, beaches, and coastline.

Lahemaa National Park is home to a wide variety of plant and animal life. Some of the most common animals in the park include moose, deer, wild boars, foxes, and hares. The park is also home to a number of rare and endangered species, such as the Eurasian lynx and the white-tailed eagle.

There are a number of things to do in Lahemaa National Park. Visitors can go hiking, biking, swimming, boating, and fishing in the park. There are also a number of historical and cultural attractions in the park, including manor houses, churches, and windmills.

Some of the most popular tourist destinations in Lahemaa National Park include:

• **Palmse Manor:** This 18th-century manor house is one of the most popular tourist attractions in the park. The manor house is surrounded by a beautiful park, and it is home to a number of museums.

• **Sagadi Manor:** This 19th-century manor house is another popular tourist destination in the park.

The manor house is surrounded by a forest, and it is home to a number of museums and hiking trails.

- **Viru Bog:** This bog is one of the largest in Estonia, and it is a popular destination for hiking and bird watching.

- **Käsmu:** This village is located on the coast of the Gulf of Finland, and it is known for its beautiful beaches and its traditional wooden houses.

- **Altja:** This village is located on the coast of the Gulf of Finland, and it is known for its mediaeval ruins and its traditional fishing culture.

Lahemaa National Park is a great place to visit for a relaxing vacation or an exciting adventure. The park has something to offer everyone, and it is a great place to experience the natural beauty of Estonia.

Here are some additional tips for planning your trip to Lahemaa National Park:

- The best time to visit the park is during the summer, when the weather is warm and sunny.
- There are a number of different places to stay in the park, including hotels, guesthouses, and campsites.
- There are a number of different ways to get to Lahemaa National Park, including by car, bus, and train.
- The park has a number of different hiking trails, so you can choose a trail that is appropriate for your fitness level.
- Be sure to bring insect repellent, as there can be a lot of mosquitoes in the park during the summer.

Hiiumaa Island

Hiiumaa is the second largest island in Estonia, and it is known for its beautiful nature, rich history, and charming towns. It is located in the Baltic Sea, about 22 kilometres from the Estonian mainland. The island has an area of 989 square kilometres and is home to about 10,000 people.

Some of the top destinations in Hiiumaa include:

• **Kõpu Lighthouse:** This is one of the oldest lighthouses in the world, and it is located on the western coast of the island. The lighthouse was built in 1531, and it is still in operation today.

• **Tahkuna Lighthouse:** This is the tallest lighthouse in Estonia, and it is located on the northern coast of the island. The lighthouse was built in 1874, and it is a popular tourist destination.

• **Ristna Beach:** This is one of the most beautiful beaches in Estonia, and it is located on the southern coast of the island. The beach is well-known for its white sand and crystal-clear water.

- **Kassari Chapel:** This is a small chapel that is located on the island of Kassari. The chapel was built in the 17th century, and it is one of the most popular tourist attractions in Hiiumaa.

- **Orjaku Tower:** This is a bird watching tower that is located on the island of Orjaku. The tower offers stunning views of the surrounding countryside, and it is a popular spot for bird watching.

- **Hiiumaa Museum:** This museum is located in the town of Kärdla, and it tells the story of Hiiumaa's history and culture. The museum has exhibits on the island's prehistoric inhabitants, its mediaeval history, and its role in the Estonian War of Independence.

In addition to these popular destinations, there are many other things to see and do in Hiiumaa. You can go hiking or biking in the forests, visit the many farms and manor houses, or take a boat trip to one of the island's many islets. There are also plenty of opportunities to try local food and drink, such as the island's famous smoked fish and beer.

Here are some additional facts about Hiiumaa:

- The island is home to a number of protected areas, including the Tahkuna Nature Reserve and the West Estonian Archipelago Biosphere Reserve.
- Hiiumaa is a popular destination for birdwatchers, as it is home to over 250 species of birds.
- The island is also known for its production of smoked fish and beer.

• Hiiumaa is a popular destination for Estonians, and it is often referred to as "the summer capital of Estonia."

Viljandi

Viljandi is a charming town located in southern Estonia. It is known for its beautiful architecture, lively cultural scene, and proximity to nature. Here are some of the top things to see and do in Viljandi:

• **Viljandi Castle:** The ruins of Viljandi Castle are one of the most popular tourist attractions in the town. The castle was built in the 13th century and was once one of the most important fortifications in Estonia.

• **Viljandi Town Hall:** The Viljandi Town Hall is a beautiful example of Renaissance architecture. The town hall was built in the 16th century and is now a museum.

- **Viljandi Lake:** Viljandi Lake is a popular spot for swimming, boating, and fishing. A variety of bird species can also be seen around the lake.

- **Viljandi Music Festival:** The Viljandi Music Festival is one of the largest folk music festivals in Europe. The festival is held every July and attracts thousands of people from all over the world.

- **Viljandi Culture Academy:** The Viljandi Culture Academy is a renowned institution for the study of music, dance, and theatre. The academy offers a variety of courses and programs, both for Estonian and international students.

- **Olustvere Manor:** Olustvere Manor is a beautiful manor house located just outside of

Viljandi. The manor house was built in the 17th century and is now a hotel and conference centre.

● **Soomaa National Park:** Soomaa National Park is a beautiful national park located just south of Viljandi. The park is known for its bogs, forests, and rivers.

Here are some additional tips for planning your trip to Viljandi:

● The best time to visit Viljandi is during the summer, when the weather is warm and sunny. However, the town is also a popular destination during the winter, when the Christmas markets are in full swing.
● Viljandi is a small town, so you can easily walk or bike around. However, there is also a good public transportation system in place.

- There are a variety of accommodation options available in Viljandi, from budget-friendly hostels to luxury hotels.
- There are many restaurants in Viljandi serving traditional Estonian food, as well as international cuisine.
- Viljandi is a great place to experience Estonian culture. There are a number of museums, theatres, and music venues in the town.

Rakvere

Rakvere is a town in northern Estonia, and it is the administrative centre of Lääne-Viru County. It is a popular tourist destination, and it is known for its historical sites, museums, and cultural events.

Rakvere was founded in the 13th century, and it was originally a stronghold of the Teutonic Order. The town was destroyed by fire in the 16th century, but it was rebuilt and became an important centre of trade and commerce. In the 19th century, Rakvere became a popular resort town, and it was known for its mineral springs.

Top Attractions in Rakvere worth visiting for tourists includes

• **Rakvere Castle:** This 14th-century castle is one of the most popular tourist attractions in Rakvere. It is now a museum, and you can explore the castle's towers, halls, and dungeons.

• **Town Hall:** This town hall was built in the 17th century, and it is one of the oldest surviving town halls in Estonia. It is now a museum, and you can see exhibits on the town's history and culture.

• **Pikk Hermann Tower:** This tower is the tallest structure in Rakvere, and it offers panoramic views of the town. You can climb to the top of the tower for stunning views of the surrounding area.

- **Rakvere Art Museum:** This museum houses a collection of Estonian and international art. You can see paintings, sculptures, and other works of art from the 16th century to the present day.

- **Rakvere Museum of Technology:** This museum tells the story of technology in Estonia from the 18th century to the present day. You can see exhibits on everything from steam engines to computers.

- **Rakvere Forest:** This forest is located just outside of Rakvere, and it is a popular spot for hiking, biking, and picnicking.

Other Things to Do include:

- Visit the Rakvere Beer Museum and learn about the history of beer brewing in Estonia.
- Take a walk through the Old Town and admire the well-preserved architecture.
- Explore the town's numerous boutiques and gift shops.
- Enjoy a performance at the Rakvere Drama Theatre.
- Sample the local cuisine at one of Rakvere's many restaurants.

The best time to visit Rakvere is during the summer, when the weather is warm and sunny. However, the town is also a popular destination during the winter, when it is transformed into a winter wonderland.

Rakvere is located about 140 kilometres (87 miles) from Tallinn, the capital of Estonia. You can get to Rakvere by train, bus, or car. The train journey from Tallinn takes about 2 hours, and the bus journey takes about 1 hour and 30 minutes.

CHAPTER 6: ESTONIAN CUISINE AND DINING

Estonian cuisine is a delightful blend of traditional Nordic, German, Russian, and Scandinavian influences, all shaped by the country's natural resources and historical context. Estonia boasts of a rich culinary heritage with an emphasis on simple, hearty, and locally sourced ingredients. Estonian cuisine is characterised by its use of grains, potatoes, dairy products, fish, and wild game, all of which are staples in the traditional diet.

Traditional Estonian Dishes

Estonian food is a hearty and flavorful blend of European cuisines. If you are looking for a delicious and authentic Estonian meal, be sure to try some of these traditional dishes.

Key Ingredients and Influences:

1. Fish: Being a country with an extensive coastline and numerous rivers and lakes, fish is an essential part of Estonian cuisine. Popular fish varieties include Baltic herring, salmon, perch, and flounder.

2. Potatoes: Potatoes play a significant role in Estonian meals and are often used as a side dish or as part of hearty stews and soups.

3. Grains: Rye, wheat, and barley are common grains used in Estonian cuisine, with rye being particularly important. Estonians are known for their dark, dense rye bread, which is a staple on many dining tables.

4. Dairy: Dairy products like milk, buttermilk, sour cream, and various cheeses are widely consumed. Sour cream, in particular, is a beloved condiment and a key ingredient in many traditional dishes.

5. Wild Game: Hunting is a traditional activity in Estonia, and as a result, wild game like elk, boar, and deer often find their way onto restaurant menus and family dinners.

6. Forest Berries and Mushrooms: The country's abundant forests provide a variety of berries, such as blueberries, lingonberries, and cranberries, along with wild mushrooms that are cherished ingredients in Estonian cuisine.

7. Pickled and Preserved Foods: In line with their Nordic neighbours, Estonians have a penchant for pickling and preserving foods like cucumbers, cabbage, and herring.

Traditional Estonian Dishes

1. Estonian Black Bread (Leib): A dense and hearty rye bread, typically baked in large loaves, which has a slightly sweet and nutty flavour.

2. Verivorst: Blood sausages made from a mixture of pork blood, barley, and spices, often served with lingonberry sauce.

3. Mulgipuder: A comforting dish made from potatoes and barley groats, usually accompanied by a flavorful sauce and traditionally enjoyed in the Mulgimaa region.

4. Kartulipuder: Mashed potatoes that often accompany meat dishes or stews.

5. Kiluvõileib: An open-faced sandwich featuring marinated Baltic herring, often served with boiled eggs, cucumber, and tomato slices.

6. Rosolje: A salad made from boiled and diced potatoes, beets, carrots, pickles, and herring, mixed with sour cream.

7. Hapukapsasupp: Sauerkraut soup with pork, potatoes, carrots, and spices, offering a savoury and tangy flavour.

8. Vürtsikilu: (spicy sprats) are a popular Estonian appetiser. They are made with small herring that have been marinated in a spicy sauce.

9. Pea soup: is a popular Estonian soup made with peas, smoked pork, and spices. It is a hearty and warming dish that is perfect for a cold day.

10. Vürtsikilu: (spicy sprats) are a popular Estonian appetiser. They are made with small herring that have been marinated in a spicy sauce.

Estonian Dining Culture

Estonians take pride in their dining culture, which is rooted in simplicity, hospitality, and enjoying meals with family and friends. Here are some key aspects of Estonian dining culture:

1. Sauna and Food: Sauna culture is an integral part of Estonian life, and it is common to enjoy hearty meals and refreshing beverages after a sauna session.

2. Seasonal Eating: Estonians embrace seasonal ingredients, and many dishes are prepared according to the produce available during specific times of the year.

3. Preserving Traditions: Traditional dishes, especially those associated with holidays and celebrations, are cherished and passed down through generations.

4. Foraging: Foraging for berries, mushrooms, and herbs in the forests is a popular activity, and many Estonians take pride in using these fresh, local ingredients in their cooking.

5. Festive Cuisine: During holidays like Christmas and Midsummer's Eve, special meals are prepared, often featuring dishes like roasted pork, blood sausages, and various pastries.

Estonian Beverages

1. Kali: A non-alcoholic fermented beverage made from malt, rye bread, and yeast, offering a slightly sweet and tangy taste.

2. Kvass: A traditional fermented drink made from rye bread, water, sugar, and yeast, similar to kali.

3. Vana Tallinn: Estonia's famous liqueur, featuring a blend of rum, citrus, and various spices, perfect for sipping or adding to desserts.

Estonian Desserts

Estonian cuisine is also known for its desserts, which are often made with fresh fruits and berries. Some popular Estonian desserts include:

1. Kringel: A delicious Estonian sweet bread similar to a cinnamon roll but often braided and topped with pearl sugar and almonds.

2. Kama: A traditional Estonian dessert made from a mixture of roasted barley, rye, oats, and peas, served with sour cream or yoghurt.

3. Kohuke: A popular sweet treat, consisting of quark (curd cheese) covered in chocolate.

4. Vastlakukkel: is a traditional Estonian pastry that is made with a sweet dough and filled with whipped cream and jam. It is often served during the Shrovetide season.

5. Rhubarb Biscuit Cake: is a delicious cake made with rhubarb, biscuits, and whipped cream. It is a perfect summer dessert.

6. Baked Apples: are a simple but delicious dessert that is made with apples that have been baked in the oven with sugar and spices.

Here are some tips for dining in Estonia:

• Estonian restaurants typically serve large portions. If you are not a big eater, you may want to order a half portion.

- Estonian food is often served with a side of bread. If you are not a fan of bread, you can ask for it to be left off your plate.
- Estonian restaurants typically offer a variety of alcoholic beverages. If you are not a drinker, you can ask for a glass of water or juice.
- Estonian restaurants are generally very welcoming to tourists. If you have any questions about the menu or the food, do not hesitate to ask your server.

Imagine enjoying a warm meal with family or discovering the diverse flavours of the Estonian landscape, the country's cuisine is sure to leave a lasting impression on any food enthusiast.

Popular Restaurants and Cafés

Estonia's vibrant culinary scene reflects the country's rich history, diverse influences, and an emphasis on using fresh, local ingredients. From cozy cafés to fine dining establishments, there is something to suit every palate. Let's take a gastronomic journey through some of the popular restaurants and cafés in Estonia:

Popular Restaurants

1. Restoran ORE

- Location: Rotermanni 2, Tallinn
- Cuisine: Modern European, Nordic
- Overview: ORE is a renowned fine dining restaurant that offers a modern and innovative approach to Nordic cuisine. Led by Chef Silver Saa, the restaurant focuses on seasonal ingredients sourced from local farmers and foragers. The menu changes frequently to reflect the freshest produce available, ensuring a delightful surprise with every visit.

2. Rataskaevu 16

- Location: Rataskaevu 16, Tallinn
- Cuisine: Estonian, European

- Overview: Situated in Tallinn's mediaeval Old Town, Rataskaevu 16 is a charming restaurant that serves classic Estonian dishes with a contemporary twist. The cozy ambiance and friendly staff create a welcoming atmosphere for guests to enjoy local favourites like mulgipuder (potato and barley porridge), elk soup, and mouthwatering desserts.

3. Leib Resto ja Aed

- Location: Uus 31, Tallinn
- Cuisine: Estonian, Nordic
- Overview: Leib Resto ja Aed (Bread Restaurant and Garden) is a popular dining spot that celebrates traditional Estonian flavours and organic ingredients. The restaurant's highlight is its delicious homemade bread, and their seasonal menus showcase the best of Estonia's produce and culinary heritage.

4. NOP - Nordic Organic Food & Drink

- Location: Telliskivi 60A, Tallinn
- Cuisine: Organic, Vegetarian-Friendly
- Overview: NOP is a trendy and eco-conscious restaurant that places a strong emphasis on organic and locally sourced ingredients. Their menu is designed to cater to various dietary preferences, including vegetarian and vegan options. The restaurant's sustainable approach to dining has earned it a loyal following among locals and visitors alike.

5. F-hoone

- Location: Telliskivi 60E, Tallinn
- Cuisine: European, Contemporary
- Overview: Housed in a former industrial complex, F-hoone boasts a unique and stylish setting. The restaurant's menu is diverse, featuring everything from burgers and salads to hearty meat dishes. It's a

popular spot for brunch on weekends, offering a relaxed and artsy atmosphere.

Other popular restaurants worth visiting in Estonia include:

- **Taevas is a rooftop restaurant located in Tallinn.** It offers stunning views of the city and a menu of modern Estonian cuisine.

- **KGB Restaurant** is a former KGB headquarters that has been converted into a restaurant. It offers a menu of Estonian and Russian dishes, as well as a tour of the former KGB headquarters.

- **Mimosa is a Russian restaurant located in Tallinn.** It offers a wide variety of Russian dishes, such as pelmeni (dumplings), borscht (beet soup), and chicken Kiev.

- **Noa is a seafood restaurant located in Tallinn.** It offers a wide variety of fresh seafood dishes, including grilled fish, lobster, and oysters.

- **Olde Hansa** is a mediaeval-themed restaurant located in Tallinn. It offers traditional Estonian dishes such as verivorst (blood sausage) and mulgikapsad (sauerkraut stew).

Popular Cafés

1. Café Maiasmokk

- Location: Pikk 16, Tallinn
- Cuisine: Café, Pastries
- Overview: Café Maiasmokk, established in 1864, holds the title of being the oldest operating café in Tallinn. Stepping inside feels like a journey back in time, with its historic interior and elegant decor. It is famous for its delectable pastries, marzipan creations, and aromatic coffee.

2. Pegasus

- Location: Harju 1, Tallinn
- Cuisine: Café, International
- Overview: Pegasus is a beloved café located in the heart of Tallinn. It is known for its vast selection of cakes and pastries, making it an ideal spot for sweet indulgence. The café also offers a range of savoury dishes, making it a perfect place for a leisurely lunch or afternoon tea.

3. Werner Café

- Location: Vene 10, Tartu
- Cuisine: Café, European
- Overview: Werner Café in Tartu is a charming and cozy place with a warm ambiance. The café's menu features a mix of international and Estonian dishes, as well as a variety of cakes and desserts. It's a popular spot for locals and visitors seeking a relaxed setting to enjoy good food and company.

Other popular Cafés you need to explore includes:

- **Värava Cafe is located in Tallinn's Old Town.** It is a popular spot for locals and tourists alike. The cafe offers a variety of coffees, teas, pastries, and sandwiches.

- **Must Puudel is located in Tallinn's Kalamaja neighbourhood.** It is a popular spot for coffee, pastries, and brunch. The cafe is known for its mustikas (blueberry) pancakes and its kohvikoort (whipped cream).

- **Koogimeister is located in Tartu.** It is a popular spot for coffee, pastries, and cakes. The cafe is known for its kook (cake) selection, which includes both traditional Estonian cakes and more modern cakes.

Estonia's culinary landscape offers a delightful array of dining options, from high-end restaurants celebrating Nordic cuisine to cozy cafés showcasing traditional flavours and sweet treats. Whether you're exploring the mediaeval streets of Tallinn or venturing to other cities in the country, you'll find a plethora of popular restaurants and cafés that cater to all tastes, making your gastronomic journey through Estonia truly unforgettable.

CHAPTER 7: FESTIVALS AND EVENTS IN ESTONIA

Estonia's calendar is filled with a diverse array of festivals and events, reflecting the country's rich cultural heritage and strong sense of community. From music and dance celebrations to seasonal festivities, each event showcases Estonia's unique traditions and offers an immersive experience for locals and visitors alike. Below are some of the most significant festivals and events in Estonia, along with their specific dates and brief descriptions of how they are celebrated:

Song and Dance Celebration

The Estonian Song and Dance Celebration is a massive choral festival that is held every 4-5 years. The festival features over 30,000 singers from all over Estonia, and it is one of the largest choral events in the world. The festival is a celebration of

Estonian culture and identity, and it is a time for people from all over Estonia to come together and sing.

The first Song and Dance Celebration was held in 1869, and it has been held every 4-5 years ever since. The festival is always held in Tallinn, and it typically lasts for 5 days. The festival features a variety of choral performances, as well as folk dancing, music, and theatre.

The Song and Dance Celebration is a very important event for Estonians, and it is a source of great pride. The festival is a reminder of Estonia's rich cultural heritage, and it is a symbol of Estonian unity.

Midsummer's Eve (Jaaniõhtu)

Midsummer's Eve is the most important festival in Estonia, and it is celebrated with bonfires, dancing, and singing. The festival is a time for families and friends to gather and celebrate the summer solstice.

Midsummer's Eve is celebrated on June 23-24, and it is a time for Estonians to come together and celebrate the longest day of the year. The festival is a time for people to connect with nature, and it is a time for people to enjoy the company of their loved ones.

On Midsummer's Eve, Estonians traditionally build bonfires, dance around the bonfires, and sing traditional songs. They also eat traditional foods such as herring, potatoes, and strawberries.

Midsummer's Eve is a magical time in Estonia, and it is a time for people to let loose and have fun.

Tallinn Christmas Market

The Tallinn Christmas Market is a popular Christmas market that is held in Tallinn every year. The market features stalls selling traditional Christmas food, drinks, and gifts.

The Tallinn Christmas Market is a great place to experience the Christmas spirit in Estonia. The market is always festively decorated, and there is always a lot of activity. There are also often live music performances at the market.

The Tallinn Christmas Market is open from late November to December 24. It is a great place to buy Christmas presents, and it is also a great place to just wander around and enjoy the atmosphere.

Other festivals and events in Estonia worth attending for tourists alike include:

- **Viljandi Folk Music Festival (Viljandi pärimusmuusika festival)**

The Viljandi Folk Music Festival is a celebration of traditional folk music and culture held in the picturesque town of Viljandi in late July. The festival attracts musicians and performers from Estonia and around the world, showcasing a diverse range of folk music styles. Concerts, workshops, and dance performances take place in various venues throughout the town. The festival's friendly and laid-back atmosphere allows visitors to immerse themselves in the vibrant world of folk music and connect with Estonia's cultural heritage.

- **Pärnu Weekend Festival (Pärnu Weekend Festival)**

The Pärnu Weekend Festival is an annual electronic dance music (EDM) event held in the coastal town of Pärnu in Mid - August. It draws music lovers and party-goers for a weekend of energetic performances by top international and local DJs. The festival features various stages, each offering a different genre of electronic music. The lively and vibrant atmosphere makes it a popular destination for those seeking a memorable summer music festival experience.

- **Seto Kingdom Day (Seto Kuningriigi Päev)**
Held in early August, the Seto Kingdom Day celebrates the unique cultural heritage of the Seto people, an ethnic minority living in southeastern Estonia. The event takes place in the town of Värska and includes colourful processions, traditional songs, dances, and rituals. Visitors can experience the distinct Seto culture, including their distinctive clothing, handicrafts, and culinary traditions. Seto Kingdom Day is a delightful opportunity to learn about this fascinating community and their ancient customs.

- **Tallinn Black Nights Film Festival held every November.** This is one of the largest film festivals in Northern Europe, and it attracts over 100,000 visitors each year. The festival features a wide variety of films from around the world, including feature films, shorts, documentaries, and animation.

- **Harju County is held every June.** Harju County Days is a festival that celebrates the culture and traditions of Harju County, which is the most populous county in Estonia. The festival features traditional Harju County music, dance, and food.

Estonia's festivals and events are a true reflection of the nation's cultural richness and strong sense of identity. Whether it's the grand celebration of the Song and Dance Celebration, the ancient traditions of Midsummer's Eve, the festive atmosphere of the Tallinn Christmas Market, or the vibrant music gatherings, each event offers an immersive and unforgettable experience, providing a glimpse into the heart and soul of Estonia. Visitors to these festivals can witness the country's deep-rooted cultural heritage and witness the warmth and hospitality of its people.

CHAPTER 8: FUN THINGS TO DO

Despite being one of the smallest countries in the Baltic region, Estonia is abundant with natural beauty and offers a plethora of thrilling outdoor activities for adventure seekers and nature lovers alike. From pristine forests and serene lakes to rugged coastlines and charming islands, this enchanting country has something to offer every outdoor enthusiast. So, grab your gear and get ready for an unforgettable journey into the wilderness of Estonia!

Hiking and Trekking

Estonia boasts an extensive network of hiking trails that crisscross its diverse landscapes. One of the most renowned hiking routes is the Oandu-Ikla trail, a 375 km long path that takes you through lush forests, marshlands, and coastal cliffs. For those seeking a shorter but equally rewarding hike, the Soomaa National Park offers picturesque boardwalks through wetlands and dense forests. Additionally, the Viru bog and Alutaguse are perfect for nature enthusiasts looking to experience Estonia's unique wilderness. Other places you can also go hiking are Karula National Park, Lahemaa National Park and Otepää.

Trekking is a great way to explore the more remote parts of Estonia. Some of the most popular trekking destinations in Estonia include: Kõrvemaa National Park and Virumaa Highlands.

Cycling Adventures

With its flat terrain and well-maintained bike paths, Estonia is a cyclist's paradise. Travel through charming villages, scenic coastal routes, and picturesque countryside as you pedal along the country's numerous cycling trails. There are many different cycling routes to choose from, ranging from easy family-friendly routes to challenging multi-day treks.

Some of the most popular cycling destinations in Estonia include:

- **Võru-Vormsi cycling route:** This is a 300-kilometre (186-mile) route that takes you from Võru County in the south to Vormsi Island in the west. The route passes through a variety of different landscapes, including forests, lakes, and farmland.

- **Valga-Uulu cycling route:** This is a 150-kilometre (93-mile) route that takes you from Valga County in the south to Uulu Beach in the north. The route passes through Valga-Tartu County, which is known for its rolling hills and forests.

- **Tallinn-Narva cycling route:** This is a 200-kilometre (124-mile) route that takes you from the capital city of Tallinn to the Russian border town of Narva. The route passes through Harju County, which is known for its beaches, forests, and historical sites.

- **Kuressaare-Tolkuse cycling route:** This is a 70-kilometre (43-mile) route that takes you from the Saaremaa Island to the Tolkuse Manor in the mainland. The route passes through a variety of different landscapes, including forests, lakes, and farmland.

- **RMK cycling routes:** The Estonian Forest Service (RMK) has developed a network of over 1,000 kilometres (621 miles) of cycling trails throughout Estonia. These trails are well-maintained and offer a variety of different difficulty levels.

No matter what your level of experience or fitness, you're sure to find a cycling route in Estonia that's perfect for you if you decide to explore the country on two wheels!

Here are some tips for cycling in Estonia:

1. Plan your route in advance: There are many different cycling routes to choose from, so it's important to plan your route in advance. This will help you to choose a route that is appropriate for your level of experience and fitness.

2. Be aware of the terrain: Estonia is a flat country, but there are some hills and forests that you will need to be aware of. If you are not used to cycling in hilly terrain, it is a good idea to choose a route that avoids hills.

3. Wear appropriate clothing: Estonia can be cold in the winter and hot in the summer, so it is important to wear appropriate clothing for the weather. You should also wear comfortable shoes that are designed for cycling.

4. Bring water and snacks: It is important to bring water and snacks with you when you are cycling. This will help you to stay hydrated and energised during your ride.

5. Be aware of traffic: Estonia has a good network of cycling paths, but there are also some roads that you will need to share with cars. Be sure to be aware of traffic when you are cycling on roads.

Water Sports

Estonia's coastline and abundant lakes provide excellent opportunities for water sports enthusiasts. Engage in thrilling activities such as kayaking, canoeing, and stand-up paddleboarding along the serene lakes and rivers. For those seeking more adventurous experiences, sailing trips in the Baltic Sea or around the charming islands of Hiiumaa and Saaremaa are highly recommended.

Here are some of the water sports adventures available in Estonia:

1. Surfing: Estonia's long coastline and exposed beaches make it a great place for surfing. The best time to surf in Estonia is during the summer months, when the waves are at their best. Some popular surfing spots include Pärnu Beach, Haapsalu Beach, and Kärdla Beach.

2. Windsurfing: Windsurfing is another popular water sport in Estonia. The best time to windsurf in Estonia is during the summer months, when the winds are strong and steady. Some popular windsurfing spots include Pärnu Bay, Haapsalu Bay, and Matsalu Bay.

3. Kitesurfing: Kitesurfing is a relatively new water sport that is becoming increasingly popular in Estonia. The best time to kitesurf in Estonia is during the summer months, when the winds are strong and the waves are small. Some popular kitesurfing spots include Pärnu Bay, Haapsalu Bay, and Matsalu Bay.

4. Stand Up Paddleboarding: Stand Up Paddleboarding (SUP) is a great way to explore Estonia's waterways. SUP boards are easy to paddle, and they can be used on both lakes and rivers. Some popular SUP spots include Lake Võrtsjärv, the Pärnu River, and the Narva River.

5. Kayaking: Kayaking is a great way to explore Estonia's coastline and waterways. Kayaks are easy to manoeuvre, and they can be used on both flat water and in whitewater. Some popular kayaking spots include the Võhandu River, the Pärnu River, and the Soomaa National Park.

6. Canoeing: Canoeing is similar to kayaking, but canoes are typically larger and more stable. Canoes are a good option for people who are new to paddling, or for people who want to explore Estonia's waterways with a group of friends or family.

7. Sailing: Sailing is a great way to see Estonia from a different perspective. There are many different sailing routes available, from short day trips to longer overnight excursions. Some popular sailing spots include Pärnu Bay, Haapsalu Bay, and the Gulf of Finland.

Wildlife Watching

Estonia is home to an array of unique wildlife species, making it a perfect destination for wildlife enthusiasts. Explore the Lahemaa National Park, Estonia's largest national park, where you can spot various animals like moose, wild boar, and even brown bears if you're lucky. Birdwatchers will find paradise in the Matsalu National Park, a renowned bird migration hotspot.

Winter Sports

When winter arrives, Estonia transforms into a wonderland for winter sports enthusiasts. Embrace the cold with thrilling activities such as cross-country skiing, snowshoeing, and even ice climbing. The Otepää region is particularly famous for its winter sports facilities and opportunities.

Here are some of the winter sports adventures available in Estonia:

1. Skiing: Estonia has a number of ski resorts, ranging from small family-friendly resorts to large resorts with international acclaim. Some popular ski resorts in Estonia include:

• **Otepää Ski Resort:** This is the largest ski resort in Estonia, and it offers a variety of slopes for all levels of skiers and snowboarders.

• **Elva Ski Resort:** This is a smaller ski resort that is located close to the city of Tartu. It is a great option for families and beginners.

• **Kuressaare Ski Resort:** This is a ski resort located on the island of Saaremaa. It is a great option for those who want to combine skiing with a beach vacation.

2. Snowboarding: Estonia is a great place to go snowboarding, with plenty of snow and well-maintained trails. Most of the ski resorts in Estonia also offer snowboarding facilities.

3. Ice skating: Estonia has many frozen lakes and rivers that are perfect for ice skating. Some popular ice skating destinations include:

• **The Freedom Square in Tallinn:** This is a large square in the heart of Tallinn that is turned into an ice rink during the winter months.

• **Kadriorg Park in Tallinn:** This is a beautiful park in Tallinn that is home to a large ice rink.

• **The Pärnu Beach:** This is a popular beach in Pärnu that is also home to an ice rink during the winter months.

4. Snowmobiling: Snowmobiling is a great way to explore the Estonian countryside in winter. There are a number of snowmobile trails that are open to the public, and there are also a number of companies that offer snowmobile tours.

5. Winter hiking: Winter hiking is a great way to enjoy the beauty of the Estonian countryside in winter. There are a number of hiking trails that are open in winter, and there are also a number of companies that offer winter hiking tours.

Rock Climbing

For rock climbers, the Lahemaa National Park and the Ontika cliffs offer exciting challenges and breathtaking views. Whether you are a beginner or an experienced climber, Estonia has something to suit all skill levels. It is a great place for rock climbing, with over 1,000 different climbing spots. Estonia is also home to a number of climbing schools and guides, so it is a great place to learn how to climb.

Some of the most popular rock climbing areas in Estonia include:

1. Pohjumägi: This is a popular spot for bouldering, with over 1,000 different problems to choose from.

2. Ruhnu Island: This island has some of the best sea cliff climbing in Estonia.

3. Vilsandi National Park: This park has a variety of climbing terrain, including sea cliffs, boulders, and overhangs.

4. Soomaa National Park: This park is home to some of the most challenging multi-pitch routes in Estonia.

If you are looking for a rock climbing adventure in Estonia, there are a few things you should keep in mind:

- The best time to climb in Estonia is during the summer months, when the weather is warm and dry.
- Some of the climbing areas in Estonia can be remote, so it is important to be prepared for anything.
- There are a number of climbing schools and guides in Estonia, so you can get help if you need it.

Horseback Riding

Experience the beauty of Estonia's countryside on horseback. There are various riding stables and equestrian centres that offer guided tours through forests, meadows, and along the coastline, providing a unique perspective of the country's natural beauty.

Here is some information about horseback riding adventures in Estonia:

- Estonia has a long history of horse riding, and there are many opportunities to go horseback riding in the country. Some popular horse riding destinations include the Soomaa National Park, the Karula National Park, and the Lahemaa National Park.

• There are a variety of horse riding trails available in Estonia, ranging from easy rides to challenging treks. Riders of all levels can find a trail that is right for them.

• Horseback riding is a great way to explore Estonia's beautiful countryside and wildlife. Riders can often see deer, elk, and other animals while they are riding.

• Horseback riding is also a great way to experience Estonian culture. Many of the horse riding stables in Estonia offer traditional Estonian meals and drinks.

Here are some of the benefits of horseback riding adventures in Estonia:

- It is a great way to get exercise. Horseback riding is a low-impact activity that is good for your cardiovascular health.

- It is a great way to connect with nature. Horseback riding allows you to experience the beauty of Estonia's countryside from a unique perspective.

- It is a great way to learn about Estonian culture. Many of the horse riding stables in Estonia offer traditional Estonian meals and drinks.

- It is a great way to make new friends. Horseback riding is a social activity, and you are likely to meet other people who share your interests.

If you are looking for an adventure in Estonia, horseback riding is a great option. There are many opportunities to ride in beautiful natural surroundings, and you will have the chance to learn about Estonian culture and meet new people.

Here are some tips for planning a horseback riding adventure in Estonia:

- Choose a reputable horse riding stable. There are many horse riding stables in Estonia, so it is important to choose one that has a good reputation.
- Decide what type of experience you want. There are different types of horseback riding experiences available in Estonia, so decide what you are looking for before you book your trip.
- Be prepared for the weather. Estonia has a temperate climate, but the weather can change quickly, so pack things essential for different types for weather conditions.

Island Adventures

Estonia boasts over 2,000 islands, each with its own charm and allure. Take a ferry to Saaremaa and explore the picturesque Kaali Meteorite Crater, or visit Hiiumaa for its lighthouses, windmills, and unspoiled nature.

Adventure Parks

For adrenaline junkies and families alike, Estonia offers several adventure parks that promise exciting experiences. The Seikle Vabaks Adventure Park in Tallinn and the Meero Adventure Park in Tartu, Otepää Seikluspark is located in the Otepää National Park, Pirita Adventure Park is located in Tallinn, Nõmme Seikluspark is located in Tallinn, Vudila amusement park located in Kaiavere, Lottemaa is a theme park located in Reiu. They all feature various obstacle courses, zip lines, and climbing walls for all ages to enjoy.

Camping and Bonfires

Estonia is a camping enthusiast's dream come true. Take advantage of the country's 'everyman's right,' which allows you to camp in most uncultivated areas for up to 24 hours without permission. There are also numerous official camping sites, particularly near the lakes and coastal areas, where you can set up your tent and enjoy a cozy bonfire under the starry skies.

No matter your age or level of experience, Estonia's outdoor activities and adventures will undoubtedly leave you with cherished memories and a deep appreciation for its stunning landscapes.

CHAPTER 9: CULTURAL EXPERIENCES

As you venture into the heart of Estonia, you'll discover a world of captivating cultural experiences that reveal the country's rich heritage and traditions. Cultural experiences in Estonia are an invitation to embrace the heart and soul of the nation. Engage in the age-old ritual of saunas, where relaxation and camaraderie bring you closer to local life. Get swept away by the captivating melodies and dance steps of folk performances, where the nation's heritage comes alive in music and movement. Discover the world of skilled craftspeople, where traditional artistry thrives and stories of Estonia's culture are intricately woven into every creation. Embrace these authentic cultural experiences, and you'll find yourself connecting to Estonia's past, present, and future in a journey of discovery and wonder.

Traditional Estonian Saunas

No trip to Estonia is complete without experiencing the age-old tradition of saunas. Estonian saunas hold a special place in the hearts of locals, and this cherished ritual is deeply ingrained in the country's culture. Step into a world of soothing steam and warmth as you visit traditional saunas, often found in rural settings or near picturesque lakes. Take in the tranquil atmosphere as the heat purifies your body and soul, and after that, practise the "sauna" by cooling off in a lake or pond close by. Sauna visits frequently involve pleasant get-togethers, sincere chats, and a sense of community that leave you feeling revitalised and connected to Estonia's genuine way of life.

Folk Music and Dance Performances

Prepare to be enchanted by Estonia's vibrant folk music and dance performances, which echo with the soul of the nation. Folklore and traditions are woven into the melodies and intricate dance steps that captivate audiences. From toe-tapping reels to mesmerising choral harmonies, Estonian folk performances evoke a sense of nostalgia and pride in the country's cultural heritage. Experience these delightful spectacles at local festivals, town squares, and traditional gatherings, where the rhythm of the music and the grace of the dancers come together to tell tales of history, love, and life.

Visiting Local Craftspeople

Estonia's skilled craftspeople are the guardians of ancient craftsmanship, passing down their artistry from generation to generation. Embark on a journey to meet these masters of tradition and witness their expertise firsthand. Visit workshops where craftsmen create intricate textiles, hand-carved wooden items, and delicate ceramics. Engage with artists who breathe life into traditional patterns and designs, each telling a story that reflects Estonia's cultural roots. Take home a piece of Estonian craftsmanship as a treasured memento of your journey, knowing that it carries a piece of the country's cultural soul.

CHAPTER 10: SHOPPING IN ESTONIA

Welcome to Estonia, a shopper's haven where traditional crafts, modern fashion, and unique souvenirs beckon. Whether you're seeking handcrafted delights, stylish finds, or cherished mementos, Estonian shopping experiences offer an array of treasures to take home. Estonia's shopping scene is a delightful fusion of tradition and innovation, offering an array of retail treasures for every taste. From traditional craft markets brimming with handmade delights to chic fashion boutiques and contemporary design shops, Estonia invites you to discover unique and cherished items. Embrace the opportunity to bring home not just material souvenirs but also the memories of a retail journey that celebrates the country's rich cultural heritage and creative spirit. Whether you're browsing through the artisan workshops of the Old Town or exploring the modern convenience of shopping malls, Estonia's retail landscape promises a shopper's paradise that will leave you with cherished keepsakes and fond memories of your time in this Baltic gem.

Traditional Craft Markets

Immerse yourself in the authenticity of Estonia's traditional craft markets, where skilled artisans showcase their craftsmanship. Explore Tallinn's Old Town, where the charming Masters' Courtyard (Tallinna Käsitööõu) boasts a collection of workshops and boutiques offering handwoven textiles, exquisite ceramics, and intricate woodwork. The bustling Balti Jaam Market, located near the railway station in Tallinn, is a treasure trove of local delights, from fresh produce and vintage finds to handmade crafts and unique souvenirs. These markets offer not only the chance to buy remarkable gifts but also to engage with the talented craftsmen, gaining insights into Estonia's vibrant cultural heritage.

Fashion Boutiques

Discover Estonia's burgeoning fashion scene in the trendy boutiques of Tallinn and other major cities. Viru Street, lined with stylish shops and international brands, is a fashion lover's paradise. Kalamaja, known for its hipster vibe, showcases independent designers and up-and-coming labels that redefine fashion trends. Tartu, Estonia's intellectual heart, boasts eclectic stores with a blend of vintage treasures and contemporary pieces. Whether you're in search of cutting-edge designs or timeless classics, Estonian fashion boutiques offer an exciting shopping experience for every style enthusiast.

Design and Souvenir Shops

Bring home a piece of Estonia's creative spirit with design items and souvenirs that capture the country's essence. In Tallinn, the Telliskivi Creative City is a hub of innovation, housing design shops, studios, and galleries. Here, you'll find unique jewellery, home decor, and art pieces that showcase the talents of Estonian designers. For quintessential Estonian souvenirs, look for items featuring the country's iconic symbols, such as the folkloric rooster, the striking Vana Tallinn liqueur, and the world-famous Kalev chocolates. These cherished keepsakes are reminders of your memorable journey through Estonia.

Shopping Malls

Estonia's modern shopping malls offer a wide range of international and local brands, making them convenient destinations for retail therapy. The Viru Keskus in Tallinn's city centre houses a variety of shops, from fashion to electronics, and features a rooftop terrace with panoramic views. Ülemiste Centre, located near the airport, is one of the largest shopping centres in Estonia, offering a diverse selection of shops and entertainment options. These malls cater to all shopping preferences, providing a seamless and enjoyable experience for both visitors and locals.

Best Places to Shop

Estonia is a great place to shop for souvenirs, clothes, electronics, and other goods. Here are some of the best places to shop in Estonia:

Tallinn

- **Toompea Market:** This market is located in the Old Town of Tallinn, and it is a great place to find souvenirs, handicrafts, and local produce.

- **Viru Keskus:** This is the largest shopping mall in Tallinn, and it has a wide variety of stores, including international brands, local designers, and souvenir shops.

- **Telliskivi Creative City:** This former industrial area has been transformed into a hip and trendy shopping and arts district. There are many independent shops, boutiques, and studios selling everything from clothes and accessories to art and design.

- **Nõmme Market:** This market is located in the Nõmme district of Tallinn, and it is a great place to find fresh produce, local cheeses, and other Estonian delicacies.

Tartu

- **Kvartal:** This shopping centre is located in the heart of Tartu, and it has a mix of international brands and local shops.

- **Vanemuise Market:** This market is located in the Old Town of Tartu, and it is a great place to find souvenirs, handicrafts, and local produce.

- **Raekoja Plats:** This is the main square in Tartu, and it is surrounded by shops, cafes, and restaurants. There are also several souvenir shops selling Estonian handicrafts and souvenirs.

Other Cities

- **Pärnu:** Pärnu is a popular seaside resort town, and it has a number of shopping streets and malls. The main shopping street is Rüütli Street, which is home to a variety of shops, cafes, and restaurants.

- **Narva:** Narva is a border town with Russia, and it has a number of Russian-style shops selling souvenirs, clothes, and electronics. The main shopping street is Kreenholmi Street, which is home to a number of large department stores.

Here are some tips for shopping in Estonia:

- Bargaining is common in Estonia, so don't be afraid to haggle over prices.
- Be sure to check out the local markets, where you can find fresh produce, handicrafts, and other Estonian delicacies.
- If you are looking for souvenirs, be sure to visit the Toompea Market in Tallinn or the Nõmme Market in Tallinn.
- If you are looking for clothes, be sure to visit Viru Keskus in Tallinn or Kvartal in Tartu.
- If you are looking for electronics, be sure to visit the shops in the Telliskivi Creative City in Tallinn.

CHAPTER 11: LANGUAGE AND PHRASES BOOK

Estonian is the official language of Estonia. It is a Finno-Ugric language, which means that it is related to Finnish, Hungarian, and other languages spoken in Northern Europe. Estonian is a relatively rare language, with only about 1.1 million speakers worldwide.

Estonian Pronunciation

Estonian pronunciation can be challenging for English speakers, as there are many sounds that do not exist in English. There are, however, a few things you may do to simplify it. First, try to listen to Estonian speakers as much as possible. This will help you get a feel for the sounds of the language. Second, pay attention to the vowel sounds. Estonian has five vowel sounds, which are a, e, i, o, and u. These sounds are pronounced differently than in

English, so it is important to practise them. Finally, don't be afraid to make mistakes. Estonian speakers are usually very patient with people who are learning their language.

There are many resources available to help you learn Estonian. You can find textbooks, online courses, and even language schools that offer Estonian classes. If you are serious about learning Estonian, I recommend finding a language partner or joining a conversation group. This will give you the opportunity to practise speaking Estonian with native speakers.

Mini Estonian Phrasebook

Whether you're planning to visit Estonia for business or pleasure, having a few basic phrases in Estonian will go a long way in making connections and showing respect for the local culture. Here are some essential words and phrases to help you get started:

Greetings

1. Hello - Tere
2. Good morning - Tere hommikust
3. Good day - Tere päevast
4. Good evening - Tere õhtust
5. Goodbye - Nägemist
6. See you later - Näeme hiljem

Polite Expressions

7. Please - Palun
8. Thank you - Aitäh
9. You're welcome - Palun (in response to "thank you")
10. Excuse me / Sorry - Vabandust
11. Yes - Jah
12. No - Ei

Introductions

13. My name is... - Minu nimi on...

14. What is your name? - Mis on teie nimi?

15. Nice to meet you - Meeldiv tutvuda

Basic Conversational Phrases

16. How are you? - Kuidas läheb?

17. I'm fine, thank you - Mul läheb hästi, aitäh

18. I don't understand - Ma ei saa aru

19. Can you help me? - Kas saate mind aidata?

20. I'm sorry, I don't speak Estonian - Vabandust, ma ei räägi eesti keelt

Getting Around

21. Where is...? - Kus on...?

22. How much is this? - Kui palju see maksab?

23. Can you show me on the map? - Kas saate mulle näidata kaardil?

24. Left - Vasakule

25. Right - Paremale

Dining Out

26. I would like... - Ma sooviksin...

27. Water - Vesi

28. Coffee - Kohv

29. Tea - Tee

30. Cheers! - Terviseks!

Numbers

31. One - Üks

32. Two - Kaks

33. Three - Kolm

34. Ten - Kümme

35. Hundred - Sada

While Estonian is the official language of Estonia, you'll find that English is widely spoken and understood, especially in urban areas and popular tourist destinations. The younger generation, in particular, is well-versed in English due to its prevalence in education.

In major cities like Tallinn and Tartu, you'll find English signage in public places, restaurants, and shops. Many Estonians in the service industry, such as hotel staff, tour guides, and waiters, speak English fluently.

However, embracing a few Estonian phrases can enhance your interactions with locals and add a personal touch to your travels. The effort to learn and use the local language is always appreciated and may lead to more meaningful connections during your time in Estonia.

CHAPTER 12: PRACTICAL TIPS FOR VISITING ESTONIA

These practical tips for visiting Estonia will help you navigate daily essentials with ease during your trip. Having these tips I'm about to share with you in mind, you can focus on enjoying the beauty and cultural richness of Estonia without worrying about the practicalities of your journey. Embrace the wonders of this Baltic gem and create unforgettable memories as you explore its charming landscapes and immerse yourself in its vibrant culture.

Electrical Outlets and Voltage

When traveling to Estonia, it's essential to be prepared for the country's electrical outlets and voltage to keep your devices charged and ready. The electrical outlets in Estonia use the Type C and F plugs, which are the same as the plugs used in most European countries.

The standard voltage in Estonia is 230 volts, and the frequency is 50 Hz. If your electronic devices are compatible with this voltage, you won't need a voltage converter. However, if your devices use a different voltage, you'll need a power adapter with a built-in voltage converter to ensure safe charging.

Internet and Wi-Fi Availability

Estonia is known for its advanced and widespread internet connectivity. Whether you're in a bustling city or a tranquil rural area, you'll likely find access to reliable Wi-Fi. Many hotels, cafes, restaurants, and public spaces offer free Wi-Fi for visitors.

Additionally, Estonia is one of the first countries to provide free public Wi-Fi in many locations. Look for signs that indicate "TASUTA WIFI" (Free Wi-Fi) to connect and stay connected during your travels.

For seamless internet access while on the go, consider purchasing a local SIM card from one of the country's major mobile network providers. This will enable you to have data on your smartphone and stay connected throughout your journey.

Public Toilets and Facilities

During your travels in Estonia, you'll find public toilets and facilities readily available in cities and tourist areas. Most cafes, restaurants, shopping centres, and tourist attractions offer clean and accessible restroom facilities for their patrons.

While some public restrooms may require a small fee for usage, it's worth having some spare change handy for these instances. Look for signs that indicate "WC" (water closet) or "Toilet" to find the nearest restroom.

Keep in mind that public toilets in more remote or rural areas might be less common. Therefore, it's advisable to plan your bathroom breaks in advance when exploring off-the-beaten-path locations.

Estonian Traditions and Etiquette

Estonia, with its deep-rooted traditions and cultural heritage, holds a unique charm that captivates visitors from around the world. To fully embrace the Estonian experience and show respect for local customs, understanding the country's traditions and etiquette is essential.

Greetings and Social Norms

In general, Estonians are quiet and polite in their greetings. "Tere!" (Hello!) is the most common greeting. It is traditional to shake hands when meeting someone for the first time. If you are meeting someone in a more formal situation, you should also bow slightly.

You should be aware of a variety of social rules that apply to Estonians. For example, pointing with your finger is considered impolite. You should instead utilise your entire hand. Crossing your legs in front of someone is also considered impolite.

Gift-Giving Etiquette

Gift-giving is less common in Estonia than in other cultures. However, if you do give a present, it is critical that you select something meaningful and acceptable. Avoid offering too personal or pricey presents.

It is usual to bring a modest gift when welcomed to someone's home in Estonia. A bottle of wine or flowers are both suitable options. It's also a good idea to bring something for the host's kids.

Tipping is legal in Estonia.

Tipping is not expected, but it is valued in Estonia. If you choose to tip, a small sum is appropriate. A few euros is usually sufficient for a decent supper in a restaurant.

Here are some additional tips for etiquette in Estonia:

- Be on time. Because Estonians are very punctual, it is critical to arrive on time for appointments.
- Put on appropriate clothing. Estonians dress conservatively, therefore when visiting someone's house or attending a business meeting, it is best to dress formally.
- Personal space should be respected. Estonians want to preserve their distance from others, so avoid standing too near or invading their personal space.

- Be mindful of cultural differences. Estonia is a small country with a rich cultural and historical heritage.

Health and Medical Information

The healthcare system in Estonia is universal, meaning that all citizens and permanent residents are entitled to free healthcare. However, there are some exceptions to this rule, such as dental care and prescription medication.

If you are visiting Estonia, you will need to purchase travel insurance that covers medical expenses. This is because your home country's healthcare system will not cover you while you are in Estonia.

Common Medical Issues

The most common medical issues that visitors to Estonia experience are:

1. Traveler's diarrhoea: This is a mild form of diarrhoea that is caused by bacteria or viruses. It is usually not serious and can be treated with over-the-counter medication.

2. Colds and flu: These are common in Estonia, especially during the winter months. They can be treated with over-the-counter medication or by resting and drinking plenty of fluids.

3. Sunburn: Estonia is a sunny country, so it is important to protect yourself from the sun. So I advise you to wear sunscreen with an SPF of 30 or higher and make sure to reapply it every two hours.

4. Heatstroke: This can occur if you are not properly hydrated. Symptoms include dizziness, headache, and nausea. If you think you may be experiencing heat stroke, seek medical attention immediately.

Medical Emergencies

If you experience a medical emergency in Estonia, you should call 112 as it is the official number for the emergency services.

There are also a number of hospitals in Estonia that can provide medical care. These hospitals are located in all major cities. Such as Tartu University Hospital which is the largest hospital in Estonia and is located in Tartu and Tallinn Children'sHospital which is the main children's hospital in Estonia and is located in Tallinn.

If you need prescription medication while you are in Estonia, you will need to see a doctor. The doctor will then prescribe the medication and you will need to fill it at a pharmacy.

As mentioned earlier, it is important to purchase travel insurance that covers medical expenses before you visit Estonia. This will ensure that you are covered in case you need medical care while you are there.

Vaccinations and Health Precautions

The following vaccinations are recommended for all travellers to Estonia: Hepatitis A, Hepatitis B, Tetanus, Diphtheria and Polio.

In addition to Vaccinations, there are a few other health precautions you should take before visiting Estonia:

• **Drink bottled water:** The tap water in Estonia is safe to drink, but it is always best to err on the side of caution and drink bottled water.

- **Be aware of the risks of tick-borne diseases:** Tick-borne diseases such as Lyme disease and encephalitis are present in Estonia. Avoid contact with ticks and remove any ticks that do attach as soon as possible.
- **Stay hydrated:** Estonia can be hot in the summer, so it is important to stay hydrated. Drink plenty of fluids and avoid alcohol and caffeine.

Sustainable Travel in Estonia

Estonia is a small country with a big commitment to sustainability. The government has set ambitious goals to reduce greenhouse gas emissions and promote sustainable tourism. There are many things you can do to travel sustainably in Estonia, including:

1. Choose sustainable accommodation: There are a number of sustainable accommodation options available in Estonia, such as eco-lodges, bed and breakfasts, and farm stays. These accommodations are often located in beautiful natural areas and they use sustainable practices, such as using renewable energy and recycling.

2. Eat local food: Estonian cuisine is based on fresh, local ingredients. When you eat local food, you are helping to support local farmers and businesses and you are also reducing your carbon footprint.

3. Get around by public transportation: Estonia has a well-developed public transportation system. You can get around Tallinn and other major cities by bus, tram, or train. There are also a number of intercity buses that can take you to other parts of the country.

4. Visit nature on foot: Estonia is a beautiful country with a lot of natural beauty. There are many hiking trails and nature reserves that you can explore on foot. This is a great way to see the country and to get some exercise at the same time.

5. Pack light: When you pack light, you are reducing the amount of waste you produce. You are also making it easier to get around, as you won't have to worry about lugging heavy luggage around.

Here are some additional tips for sustainable travel in Estonia:

• **Be aware of your impact on the environment:** When you are travelling, be mindful of your impact on the environment. This means things like being careful not to litter, recycling, and choosing sustainable activities.
• **Support sustainable businesses:** There are a number of sustainable businesses in Estonia that you

can support. These businesses are working to make a difference and they deserve your support.

- **Get involved:** There are a number of ways you can get involved in sustainable tourism in Estonia. You can volunteer with an environmental organisation, attend a sustainability event, or simply spread the word about sustainable travel.

Essential Things To Pack

As you prepare for an unforgettable journey to Estonia, packing smartly will ensure you have everything you need to make the most of your experience. Whether you're exploring the enchanting cities or immersing yourself in the scenic countryside, here's a comprehensive list of essential items to include in your travel luggage:

1. Weather-Appropriate Clothing:

- Comfortable walking shoes for city strolls and outdoor adventures.

- Layered clothing to adapt to Estonia's ever-changing weather. Pack a mix of lightweight and warm layers to be prepared for any temperature.
- Waterproof jacket or coat to shield yourself from rain showers, especially during the cooler months.
- Scarf, gloves, and a hat for added warmth, especially in autumn and winter.

2. Travel Documents:

- Passport with a validity of at least six months from your planned date of departure.
- Travel visa (if required) and necessary permits.
- Printed copies and digital backups of your travel itinerary, hotel reservations, and important contact information.

3. Electrical Adapters and Chargers:

- Type F and C power adapter to charge your electronic devices in Estonian electrical outlets.

- Chargers for your phone, camera, laptop, or any other electronic devices you plan to bring.

4. Personal Medications and First-Aid Kit:

- Prescription medications with sufficient supply for the duration of your trip.
- Basic first-aid kit with bandages, antiseptic cream, pain relievers, and any necessary personal medications.

5. Personal Hygiene and Toiletries:

- Travel-sized toiletries, including shampoo, conditioner, soap, and toothpaste.
- Travel towel that dries quickly and takes up less space in your luggage.

6. Travel Backpack or Day Bag:

- A lightweight backpack for day trips and excursions.
- Packable shopping bag for eco-friendly shopping.

7. Cash and Credit Cards:

• Some cash in the local currency (Euros) for smaller purchases and places that might not accept credit cards.

• Debit/credit cards for convenience and security.

8. Travel Insurance:

• Comprehensive travel insurance that covers medical emergencies, trip cancellations, and personal belongings.

9. Travel Guidebook or Maps:

• A reliable travel guidebook or digital maps to help you navigate Estonia's attractions and cities.

10. Language Guide:

• A basic Estonian phrasebook or language guide to help you with simple greetings and communication.

11. Reusable Water Bottle:

• A reusable water bottle to stay hydrated while reducing plastic waste.

12. Camera and Binoculars:

• A camera to capture the beauty of Estonia's landscapes and memorable moments.

• Binoculars for birdwatching or getting a closer look at wildlife and scenery.

13. Sunscreen and Sunglasses:

• Sunscreen to protect your skin from the sun's rays, especially during the summer months.

• Sunglasses to protect your precious eyes from bright sunlight.

14. Snacks and Reusable Containers:

• Some favourite snacks for long journeys and in-between meals.

- Reusable containers for storing snacks or leftovers.

It is also smart to put into consideration the time of the year in which you are travelling and pack accordingly to enable you to have a comfortable and enjoyable trip to Estonia. With these essential items in your travel luggage, you'll be well-prepared to embrace the beauty of this Baltic gem, explore its captivating cities, and immerse yourself in its cultural richness.

Days	Itinerary

CHAPTER 13: TRAVELLING WITH CHILDREN IN ESTONIA

Estonia is a great place to travel with children. It is a safe and child-friendly country with plenty of activities to keep kids entertained. From captivating sights to practical services, Estonia ensures that families have a memorable and hassle-free journey. Let's explore the family-friendly side of Estonia and the available child care facilities to make your trip with little ones enjoyable.

Family-Friendly Attractions and Activities

Estonia embraces families with a variety of attractions that cater to travellers of all ages. Here are some family-friendly places and activities to include in your itinerary:

1. Lahemaa National Park: This park is home to a variety of forests, lakes, and beaches. There are plenty of hiking trails and activities for kids to enjoy.

2. Kadriorg Park: This park is located in Tallinn and is home to a number of museums, gardens, and a playground.

3. Estonian Open Air Museum: This museum is located in Rocca al Mare and is a great place to learn about Estonian culture. There are traditional houses, farms, and workshops that kids can explore.

4. Tartu Zoo: This zoo is home to a variety of animals from around the world. Kids will love seeing the lions, tigers, and bears.

5. Otepaa Adventure Park: This park is located in Otepaa and is a great place for kids to go hiking, biking, and ziplining.

6. Kidz Planet: This indoor play centre is located in Tallinn and is a great place for kids to burn off some energy. There are slides, ball pits, and other activities to keep kids entertained.

7. Minigolf: There are a number of minigolf courses in Estonia that are perfect for kids. This is a great way to spend an afternoon and get some exercise.

8. Water Parks: There are a number of water parks in Estonia that are perfect for hot summer days. Kids will love splashing around in the pools and slides.

Child Care Facilities

1. Nurseries: Nurseries are available for children aged 1-3 years old. They offer a safe and stimulating environment for children to learn and grow.

2. Kindergartens: Kindergartens are available for children aged 3-7 years old. They offer a more structured environment than nurseries and prepare children for school.

3. After-school Care: After-school care is available for children aged 6-12 years old. It provides a safe and supervised environment for children to do their homework and play.

4. Child Care Services: In major cities like Tallinn and Tartu, you can find reputable child care services, including babysitting and daycare, to provide parents with some free time for sightseeing or relaxation.

Here are some tips for travelling with children in Estonia:

- **Plan your activities:** When you are planning your trip, be sure to include activities that are appropriate for children. There are many museums, zoos, and parks in Estonia that are perfect for kids.

- **Pack the essentials:** Be sure to pack all of the essentials for your children, such as diapers, wipes, formula, snacks, and medications. You may also want to pack a stroller or carrier if you plan on doing a lot of walking.

- **Be prepared for the weather:** Estonia can have a variety of weather conditions, so be sure to pack accordingly. In the summer, it can be hot and humid, so pack light clothing and sunscreen. In the winter, it can be cold and snowy, so pack warm clothing and boots.

- **Take breaks:** Estonia is a beautiful country, but it can be tiring for kids to walk around all day. Be sure to take breaks throughout the day to let your kids rest and refuel.

- **Be patient:** Travelling with children can be challenging, but it is also a lot of fun. Be patient with your kids and try to enjoy the experience.

CHAPTER 14: ESTONIA'S UNIQUE TRAITS AND QUIRKS

Estonia, a land of captivating beauty and rich cultural heritage, boasts some truly unique traits and quirks that set it apart from other countries. As you delve into the heart of this Baltic gem, you'll uncover fascinating aspects of Estonian life that make it truly special. Let's embark on a journey of discovery to explore three of Estonia's most intriguing and distinctive features.

Sauna Culture

Sauna culture holds a significant place in Estonian life, offering a deeply ingrained tradition of relaxation, socialising, and cleansing. The sauna is not merely a place to bathe; it's a cherished ritual that transcends generations.

Estonians take immense pride in their saunas, often found in homes, summer cottages, and even in the countryside. Sauna gatherings are a common way for families and friends to come together, fostering a sense of togetherness and camaraderie.

The process typically involves sitting in the sauna's steamy heat, followed by a refreshing dip in a nearby lake or icy water, known as "sauna viht." The cleansing effect is believed to purify both the body and soul, leaving participants feeling rejuvenated and invigorated.

Sauna culture is deeply respected in Estonia, and visitors are welcomed to experience this cherished tradition. It's an opportunity to connect with the heart of Estonian life, immersing yourself in the soothing ambiance and embracing the warmth of its people.

Singing Revolution

Estonia's Singing Revolution is a testament to the power of music and unity in shaping a nation's destiny. During the late 1980s and early 1990s, as Estonia sought independence from Soviet rule, the people found solace and strength in song.

Massive gatherings known as the "Song Festivals" became symbolic acts of defiance and unity, where hundreds of thousands of Estonians would come together to sing traditional folk songs and national anthems. These peaceful demonstrations showcased the nation's determination for freedom and self-determination.

The Singing Revolution's melodic path to freedom reached a crescendo on August 23, 1989, when over two million Estonians, Latvians, and Lithuanians joined hands in the "Baltic Way," forming a human chain spanning over 600 kilometres across the three Baltic countries.

The harmonious sound of Estonian voices singing in unison became a potent force for change, eventually leading to Estonia's restoration of independence in 1991.

Virmalised (Northern Lights)

Estonia's northernmost location provides a rare and enchanting treat for those fortunate enough to witness it—the ethereal beauty of the Virmalised, or Northern Lights.

On clear winter nights, as the dark skies embrace the cold landscape, the Northern Lights paint the heavens with an enchanting display of vivid colours. Shades of green, pink, and purple dance across the sky, creating a breathtaking symphony of light.

While the Northern Lights are not as frequent or intense as in some other Arctic regions, they are still a magical sight to behold. The best chances to witness this natural spectacle are away from city lights and in areas with minimal light pollution.

Estonia's Virmalised offer a mesmerising connection to nature's wonders, inviting you to gaze at the celestial display and feel the awe-inspiring beauty of the universe.

Estonia's unique traits and quirks offer a captivating journey of discovery, revealing the country's deep-rooted traditions and extraordinary experiences. As you embrace these exceptional facets of Estonian life, you'll find yourself drawn closer to the heart and soul of this enchanting Baltic gem.

Days	Itinerary

APPENDIX

This appendix provides a valuable compilation of resources and essential information to enhance your journey and ensure a seamless travel experience.

Multiple Sample Itinerary

1. Seven days in Estonia

● **Day 1:** Arrive in Tallinn

- Explore Tallinn's Old Town, including Toompea Hill and Alexander Nevsky Cathedral.

- Visit the Town Hall Square and St. Olaf's Church.

- Enjoy a traditional Estonian dinner at a local restaurant.

● **Day 2:** Day Trip to Kadriorg and Pirita

- Visit Kadriorg Park and Kadriorg Palace.

- Explore the Estonian Art Museum and Kumu Art Museum.

- Head to Pirita Beach and enjoy the coastal views.

Day 3: Explore Tartu

- Travel to Tartu, Estonia's university town.

- Visit the University of Tartu and the Botanical Gardens.

- Explore Tartu's Old Town and Town Hall Square.

Day 4: Saaremaa Island Adventure

- Take a ferry to Saaremaa Island.

- Explore the Kuressaare Castle and the town of Kuressaare.

- Relax at Panga Cliffs and visit Kaali Meteorite Crater.

Day 5: Lahemaa National Park

- Travel to Lahemaa National Park.

- Explore Viru Bog and hike through the forest trails.

- Visit the Palmse and Sagadi Manor Houses.

Day 6: Pärnu Beach and Museum

- Head to Pärnu, Estonia's summer capital.

- Relax at Pärnu Beach and enjoy the coastal atmosphere.

- Visit the Pärnu Museum and Endla Theatre.

Day 7: Return to Tallinn

- Spend the morning in Pärnu and enjoy any last-minute sightseeing.

- Return to Tallinn for shopping and souvenir hunting.

- Depart from Tallinn and bid farewell to Estonia.

2. Sample Itinerary for Nature Enthusiasts: Exploring Estonia's Natural Beauty

● **Day 1: Arrival in Tallinn**

- Explore Tallinn's Old Town and visit Toompea Hill for panoramic views.

- Enjoy a traditional Estonian dinner at a local restaurant.

● **Day 2: Lahemaa National Park**
- Travel to Lahemaa National Park, Estonia's oldest and largest national park.
- Hike through Viru Bog and admire the stunning landscapes.
- Visit Palmse and Sagadi Manor Houses to learn about Estonia's history.

● **Day 3: Saaremaa Island Adventure**
- Take a ferry to Saaremaa Island and visit the Kuressaare Castle.
- Relax at Panga Cliffs and enjoy the serene coastal views.
- Explore Kaali Meteorite Crater, a unique natural wonder.

● **Day 4: Võru and Haanja Nature Park**

- Head to Võru and explore the charming town.

- Visit Haanja Nature Park for picturesque hiking trails and scenic views.

- Immerse yourself in the traditional Seto culture.

- **Day 5: Hiiumaa Island Retreat**
- Take a ferry to Hiiumaa Island for a peaceful getaway.

- Explore the island's lighthouses, tranquil beaches, and quaint villages.

- **Day 6: Pärnu Beach and Nature**
- Travel to Pärnu, the summer capital of Estonia.

- Relax at Pärnu Beach and enjoy the coastal ambiance.

- Visit Soomaa National Park for canoeing and exploring the floodplains.

- **Day 7: Return to Tallinn**

- Return to Tallinn for some last-minute sightseeing and shopping.
- Depart from Tallinn, cherishing the memories of Estonia's natural wonders.

3. Sample Itinerary for History and Culture Lovers: Unravelling Estonia's Heritage

• **Day 1: Arrival in Tallinn**
- Explore Tallinn's Old Town, including Toompea Hill and Alexander Nevsky Cathedral.
- Visit the Town Hall Square and St. Olaf's Church.

• **Day 2: Kadriorg Palace and Museums**
- Visit Kadriorg Park and the stunning Kadriorg Palace.
- Explore the Estonian Art Museum and Kumu Art Museum.

• **Day 3: Tartu University and Historical Sites**

- Travel to Tartu, Estonia's university town.
- Visit the University of Tartu and the Botanical Gardens.
- Explore Tartu's Old Town and Town Hall Square.

• **Day 4: Viljandi Folk Music Festival and Castle Hill**
- Experience the Viljandi Folk Music Festival (if during the festival period).
- Explore Viljandi Castle Hill and immerse yourself in folklore and history.

• **Day 5: Narva Castle and Kreenholm Manufacture**
- Head to Narva and visit the impressive Hermann Castle.
- Marvel at the panoramic views from the Kreenholm Manufacture.

• **Day 6: Valga and Valka Twin Towns**

- Explore Valga and experience the duality of two cultures.
- Visit the Valga Museum and stroll through the charming streets.

- **Day 7: Return to Tallinn**
- Return to Tallinn for some last-minute cultural experiences and souvenirs.
- Depart from Tallinn, carrying with you the rich heritage of Estonia.

4. Sample Itinerary for Family-Friendly Adventures: Fun for All Ages

- **Day 1: Arrival in Tallinn**
- Explore Tallinn's Old Town, including Toompea Hill and Alexander Nevsky Cathedral.
- Enjoy a family dinner at a local restaurant.

- **Day 2: Tallinn Zoo and Seaplane Harbour**

- Visit Tallinn Zoo to see a diverse collection of animals.
- Explore the interactive exhibits at Seaplane Harbour (Lennusadam).

• **Day 3: Tartu AHHAA Science Center**
- Travel to Tartu and spend the day at the AHHAA Science Center.
- Enjoy interactive exhibits and engaging activities for all ages.

• **Day 4: Saaremaa Adventure Park and Kuressaare Castle**
- Take a ferry to Saaremaa Island and visit the Adventure Park.
- Explore Kuressaare Castle and its mediaeval charm.

• **Day 5: Pärnu Beach and Ranna Park**

- Head to Pärnu and spend a day at the family-friendly beach.
- Visit Ranna Park for picnics and outdoor play.

- **Day 6: Estonian Open Air Museum and Kadriorg Park**
- Visit the Estonian Open Air Museum for a glimpse of rural life.
- Enjoy Kadriorg Park's beauty and have a family picnic.

- **Day 7: Return to Tallinn**
- Return to Tallinn for some last-minute family-friendly activities.
- Depart from Tallinn, cherishing the wonderful memories made in Estonia.

These itineraries are flexible and can be adjusted based on personal preferences, travel duration, and interests.

Regional Map of Estonia's Top Destinations

Here is a detailed description on the location map of Estonia's regions and top destinations. Estonia is divided into five regions:

1. Harjumaa: This is the most populous region in Estonia and is home to the capital city, Tallinn. Harjumaa is also home to a number of other popular tourist destinations, such as Kadriorg Park, the Estonian Open Air Museum, and the Lahemaa National Park.

2. Hiiumaa: This is the largest island in Estonia and is known for its beautiful beaches, forests, and traditional villages. Hiiumaa is also home to the Kärdla Town Hall, which is one of the oldest surviving wooden buildings in Estonia.

3. Ida-Virumaa: This region is located in the northeast of Estonia and is home to the Narva River, which forms the border between Estonia and Russia. Ida-Virumaa is also home to a number of industrial cities, such as Kohtla-Järve and Narva.

4. Järvamaa: This region is located in the centre of Estonia and is known for its rolling hills, forests, and lakes. Järvamaa is also home to the Paide Castle, which is one of the best-preserved mediaeval castles in Estonia.

5. Läänemaa: This region is located in the west of Estonia and is known for its beautiful beaches, forests, and historic towns. Läänemaa is also home to the Haapsalu Old Town, which is a UNESCO World Heritage Site.

Useful Websites and Resources

Here are some useful websites and resources for someone visiting Estonia:

1. Visit Estonia: The official tourism website of Estonia, offering information on attractions, events, and travel tips.

2. Estonian Tourist Board: This is another good resource for planning your trip to Estonia. It has a comprehensive website with information on tourism in Estonia, as well as a helpful toll-free number that you can call for more information.

3. Estonia Travel: This website is a good resource for finding specific things to do in Estonia. It has a comprehensive list of attractions, activities, and tours, as well as a forum where you can ask questions and get advice from other travellers.

4. Tripadvisor: This website is a great resource for finding hotels, restaurants, and other businesses in Estonia. It also has a forum where you can read reviews and ask questions from other travellers.

5. Skyscanner: This website is a good resource for finding flights to Estonia. It compares prices from a variety of airlines and travel agencies, so you can find the best deal.

6. Booking.com: This website is a good resource for finding hotels in Estonia. It has a wide variety of hotels to choose from, and you can filter your search by price, location, and amenities.

Just type these Websites in the search engine on the phone and it will provide you with the appropriate URL. Remember to check for updated information and special offers before your trip. These resources will be valuable in planning a seamless and enjoyable journey through the wonders of Estonia.

Useful (Android/iOS) Apps

When visiting Estonia, having useful apps on your smartphone can greatly enhance your travel experience and help you navigate the country with ease. Here are some must-have apps to make your trip to Estonia more enjoyable:

1. Go Mobile: This app provides information on public transportation in Estonia. You can use it to plan your trips, buy tickets, and track your journey.

2. Visit Estonia: This app is a great resource for tourists. It provides information on attractions, events, and activities in Estonia. You can also use it to book tours and accommodation.

3. Skyscanner: This app is a great way to find flights and hotels. You can compare prices from different airlines and hotels, and book your travel in advance.

4. Google Translate: This app is a lifesaver if you don't speak Estonian. It can translate text and speech between over 100 languages.

5. Citymapper: This app is a great way to get around Tallinn. It provides real-time information on public transportation, bike sharing, and taxis.

6. Maps.me: This app is a great offline map app. It provides maps of Estonia that you can use even when you don't have internet access.

7. Wolt: This app is a great way to order food delivery in Estonia. You can order from a wide variety of restaurants, and the food is usually delivered quickly.

8. Bolt: This app is a great way to get a taxi or ride-hailing service in Estonia. You can use it to book a taxi, a car, or a scooter.

This appendix serves as a valuable tool to complement your Estonian travel guide, providing essential resources and information to optimise your journey. Additionally, the list of useful websites and resources will keep you informed and equipped to make the most of your trip. With this comprehensive appendix, you're well-prepared to explore the enchanting land of Estonia and create cherished memories that will last a lifetime. Happy travels!

Days	Itinerary

CONCLUSION

Congratulations! You've reached the end of your journey through the enchanting pages of this Estonia Tourist Guide. We hope this comprehensive guide has provided you with a wealth of information, inspiring you to explore the beauty, history, and culture of this Baltic gem. From the captivating mediaeval charm of Tallinn's Old Town to the serene natural wonders of Lahemaa National Park and Saaremaa Island, Estonia has undoubtedly left an indelible mark on your heart.

We extend our heartfelt gratitude to the people of Estonia for their warm hospitality and openness in sharing their unique traditions and heritage with travellers from around the world. This guide would not have been possible without the support and collaboration of local experts, travel professionals, and cultural enthusiasts who provided invaluable insights and recommendations.

As your journey through Estonia comes to a close, we hope you depart with unforgettable memories, newfound knowledge, and a deep appreciation for this captivating country. Estonia's blend of natural beauty, rich history, and warm hospitality will forever linger in your heart.

Remember, this is not a goodbye; it's merely a **"Nägemiseni"** - until we meet again. We hope you'll return to continue your exploration of Estonia's wonders and uncover even more of its unique treasures.

From all of us who have contributed to this guide, we wish you safe travels and many more unforgettable adventures. May Estonia always hold a special place in your wanderlust-filled soul.

Thank you for choosing Estonia as your travel destination. Farewell, dear traveller, and may your future journeys be filled with magic, joy, and countless new discoveries.

Nägemiseni and safe travels!

Printed in Great Britain
by Amazon

29764823R00130